Labor Market Policies
and Employment Patterns
in the United States

Labor Market Policies and Employment Patterns in the United States

Lois Recascino Wise

Westview Press
BOULDER, SAN FRANCISCO, & LONDON

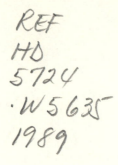

REF
HD
5724
·W5635
1989

This Westview softcover edition is printed on acid-free paper and bound in library-quality, coated covers that carry the highest rating of the National Association of State Textbook Administrators, in consultation with the Association of American Publishers and the Book Manufacturers' Institute.

Published in 1989 in the United States of America by Westview Press, Inc., 5500 Central Avenue, Boulder, Colorado 80301, and in the United Kingdom by Westview Press, Inc., 13 Brunswick Centre, London WC1N 1AF, England

First published in 1988 by EFA (The Delegation for Labor Market Policy Research, Ministry of Labor), Stockholm

Library of Congress Cataloging-in-Publication Data
Wise, Lois Recascino.
  Labor market policies and employment patterns in the United States
/ by Lois Recascino Wise.
    p. cm.
  Includes index.
  ISBN 0-8133-7839-7
  1. Labor market—United States. I. Title.
HD5724.W5635 1989
331.12'042'0973—dc20   89-32686
                                                                 CIP

Printed and bound in the United States of America

The paper used in this publication meets the requirements of the American National Standard for Permanence of Paper for Printed Library Materials Z39.48-1984.

10   9   8   7   6   5   4   3   2   1

To my parents

Contents

Figures

Tables

Acknowledgments

I am indebted to Jan Johannesson, Björn Jonzon, and Günther Schmid for ideas related to the development and structure of this study and to the responsiveness of graduate students in the School of Public and Environmental Affairs (SPEA) at Indiana University to the idea of undertaking the preliminary tasks of compiling information about programs and conditions in the United States. I value their assistance.

The former students and their areas of work are: Vivien Hertogh, public opinion and policy outcomes; Judy Jochem, labor market expenditures; Anthony Mayawa, displaced workers; Rebecca Murray, labor supply; Frank Neumann, mobility; Alfred Nhema, youth unemployment; Marie Schrup, disabled workers; Floria Thomas, female workers; and Usha Radharkrishnan, unemployment trends and market forces. More recently, I am indebted to another SPEA graduate student, Kevin Taylor, upon whose excellent research skills and diligence I have relied greatly. For the preparation of the manuscript I am indebted to Nancy Croker and Cynthia Mahigian for their generosity with their time and professional skills.

Many government officials in Washington, D.C. have provided unpublished information that allowed the study to reflect more current conditions and I am most grateful to members of the different divisions of the U.S. Department of Labor, in particular, for their assistance and for reading and commenting on the manuscript. Errors and omissions are my own responsibility.

Lois Recascino Wise
Bloomington, Indiana

Abbreviations

DOL   Department of Labor

BLS   Bureau of Labor Statistics

GAO   U.S. General Accounting Office

HHS   Department of Health and Human Services

1
Introduction

The United States lacks a comprehensive and coordinated labor market policy. The components of U.S. labor market policy are derived from the activities and programs of many different agencies and Congressional committees. In addition to the Department of Labor, major aspects of labor market policy are sponsored by the Departments of Health and Human Services and Education, and the Social Security and Veterans Administrations. There is no centralized authority over these various activities and there is no one administrative agency responsible for the implementation of active labor market policies. At the same time, states and municipalities have both the authority and the means to implement their own policies and programs to enhance the federal effort or to execute initiatives of their own. This lack of coordination not only complicates efforts to trace the course of American labor market policy, but also hampers efforts to identify the level of expenditure for labor market programs and the efficiency of program activities.

The United States has experimented with many of the same instruments that are found in other OECD countries, but there are significant differences in the methods of administration and levels of resources invested in these programs which, in turn, affect the resulting outcomes of labor market policies. There are in the United States both public and private labor market information systems to link employees with employers; there are programs for training and retraining individuals; there are programs for economically depressed regions and economically disadvantaged population groups; and there are even modest programs to provide mobility allowances and compensation for job-related relocation costs.

Absent from the American portfolio of labor market policies is significant participation on the part of organized labor or coordinated contribution from private sector employers. In the current period, more input from the private sector has been solicited but this occurs locally rather than at the national policy level. The United States lacks a centralized, uniform system; the states and territories have considerable leeway in administering federal policies as well as implementing their own programs.[1] The country lacks an efficient system for anticipating and responding to the effects of cyclical economic changes. Thus swings in duration and incidence of unemployment are apparent among different groups of workers. At the same time, there is considerable flow in and out of the work force as individuals respond to real and perceived levels of opportunity in the job market. Finally, missing from the United States is a national priority for controlling the level of unemployment and the effects of joblessness on individuals. Americans have very distinct attitudes about the causes of and responsibility for unemployment.

While job creation programs have had some popular support in the United States, employment is not perceived as an entitlement or right as, for example, social security benefits are. Public attitudes are widely distributed between two poles of opinion: one that government should see that everyone has a job and a good standard of living and the other that these are an individual's responsibility. When Americans are asked to choose between controlling the rate of inflation or unemployment, there is no clear mandate in favor of reducing unemployment. In fact, in eight surveys executed between 1975 and 1982, the majority of those polled agreed with the option: "Let prices rise and have more people unemployed."[2] This lack of public consensus is reflected in the policy making process by ambiguous laws that have more symbolic than real impact on the problem of unemployment.

According to the *Gallup Report* (April 1982) when unemployment peaked at an annual rate of 9.5 per cent of the U.S. work force in 1982, more than two-thirds of all Americans polled indicated that they thought the jobless could find work if they tried. The majority of those polled during the last recession put the responsibility for unemployment partly on the workers themselves. And a small portion (14 per cent) of the public thought that most of the jobless were out of work through their own fault. No difference was apparent among respondents who were union members.

In the current period, when fewer workers are eligible for unemployment insurance and the proportion of workers exhausting their unemployment benefits has climbed upward, the majority (52%) of Americans think that federal funding of unemployment insurance should remain at the same level. One-third of those polled in 1987 thought that the level of benefits should be increased. During periods when the rate of unemployment was higher, there was actually less support for maintaining benefit levels. In 1981, 49 per cent thought benefits should be maintained at the same levels and 23 per cent thought they should be increased.[3] It may be that as the political process appears to act on behalf of the unemployed, the proportion thinking that more should be done declines.

Since 1945, the United States has experienced eight separate recessions, as shown in Table 1.1. From 1960 to 1987, five recessionary periods are identifiable. In the last three cycles, unemployment levels at the end of the recession exceeded 7 per cent of the work force. The highest post World War II unemployment levels occurred after the most recent recession which lasted the 17 months between July 1981 and November 1982. An equally long recessionary period was observed between November 1973 and March 1975, but the unemployment rate at the end of that period was 8.6 per cent.

There is speculation about a ninth recession occurring in the United States before the end of this decade. Given this prospect, the development of U.S. labor market policy and the effectiveness of these programs are of particular interest. The question of who would weather a future economic crisis and who would be most battered by the storm can be addressed by examining employment policies for placement, job creation, and training and by reviewing existing information about the pattern of employment and unemployment in the American work force. In the following chapters, information about the U.S. labor market which is pertinent to these concerns is presented.

TABLE 1.1

Modern Recessionary Periods in the United States by Duration and Unemployment Rate

Recessionary Period	Duration in Months	Unemployment Rate[a]
November 1948 to October 1949	12	7.9
July 1953 to May 1954	11	5.9
August 1957 to April 1958	9	7.4
April 1960 to February 1961	11	6.9
December 1969 to November 1970	12	5.9
November 1973 to March 1975	17	8.6
January 1980 to July 1980	7	7.8
July 1981 to November 1982	17	10.7

[a] At end of recession.

Source: U.S. General Accounting Office, Emergency Jobs Act of 1983, December 1986.

Chapter 2 describes the policy approach of the United States to labor market conditions and provides information regarding the level of expenditures invested in different employment policy instruments. Income replacement programs are described here as well. Chapter 3 reports the supply of and demand for labor, the expansion of the public work force, and the shift in the structure of the labor market are identified. Chapter 4 describes changes in labor market dynamics related to wage differentials and mobility. The patterns of unemployment and the scope and coverage of unemployment programs are presented in Chapter 5 which documents the recent significant decline in the level of unemployment but raises questions about the job security and the risk of unemployment that workers face. Within this chapter, the effects of social disadvantage on employment status are apparent with the unemployed and underemployed more likely to be non-white, young, and female than job holders.

In Chapter 6 policy measures and programs initiated to respond to the problems of joblessness are presented. Many of these programs target specific social groups for job creation and training program activities. Finally, efforts to evaluate the effectiveness of U.S. labor market policies are presented and social and political barriers to policy impact are discussed.

2
Labor Market Policy
Instruments and Expenditures

Contemporary labor market policy in the United States can be classified into three broad stages which are not distinct from the experiences of other industrialized nations. During the 1960s, concern for the effects of automation and technological change, high rates of unemployment among certain population groups, and social unrest led to a focus on supply oriented measures to improve the employability of different segments of the work force and to increase the match between the skills required by employers and those available in the labor pool. The underlying assumption was that if the correct training and placement assistance could be administered to the jobless, they would become employed. On the one hand there was a concern for the conditions of individuals and on the other hand was an interest in the economic competitiveness of the country. Without a sufficiently skilled and modern labor force, the United States would be unable to maintain its rate of productivity and growth. At the same time, escalating rates of inflation led to pressure for an economic policy to control inflationary pressures related to labor supply and wage rates without generating unacceptably high levels of unemployment. The strategy of enhancing the quality of the work force through training was seen as an alternative economic policy.[4]

During the 1970s and into the next decade, an additional emphasis on demand oriented measures is apparent which was principally characterized by efforts to create jobs in the public sector and to provide economic incentives for hiring in business and industry. The 1980s can be distinguished by a retreat from labor market intervention on the part of the federal government and a prevalent distaste for public sector job creation. In this decade programs for training, placement, and job creation continue to exist, but the level of funding has been substantially reduced.

The impetus behind the emergence of a formal labor market policy in the United States is thus attached to three factors. First, the concern to end social unrest by improving economic opportunity and equity in resources was and continues to be a major driving force. This orientation is reflected in the number of programs aimed at persons in special groups defined by their level of disadvantage and the use of means tests to determine eligibility for program benefits. A second enduring force in the development of American labor market policies is the concern for the effects of structural change on both the level of unemployment and the competitiveness of American goods and services in world markets. Finally, a third factor is the desire to regulate the relationship between wage increases and economic inflation through improvements in the quality of the work force.

In developing a typology of labor market policy stages, many would cite the decade of the 1960s as the beginning of active labor policy in the United States. Certainly there is considerable distinction between that period and preceding years when efforts in employment and training were nominal. Yet, in comparison with the types of initiatives and resource investments that are found in other OECD countries, it is difficult to define the term "active" broadly enough to encompass the American experience. Labor market policy in the United States remains passive and reactive.

The thrust of U.S. labor market policy reflects a compensatory strategy. American efforts to address unemployment and underemployment are carried out through income replacement, training activities, and temporary jobs. The economically disadvantaged are offered various compensations for not being part of the mainstream. It is an approach that focuses on the remedial needs of persons on the periphery of the work force. It is a policy for "outsiders" rather than for those who are part of the core.[5] Economic strategy, which is not consistently integrated with labor market policy, is composed of demand oriented measures concerned with assuring economic competitiveness and growth. These measures include efforts aimed at controlling the rate of inflation and the growth of wages, limiting the rate of public expenditure, enhancing the balance of payments, and most recently, reducing the size of the public debt.

In this section, instruments of labor market policy and patterns of expenditure for labor market measures will be presented. The section begins with clearly passive efforts involving income replacement, including the large Unemployment Insurance System. The second topic pertains to government-sponsored placement activities and compensation for relocation costs. The third topic presented pertains to federal expenditures for job training and job creation activities.

2.1 Income Replacement

The principal vehicle for income replacement in the United States is the Unemployment Insurance System (UI) which was established under the Social Security Act of 1935 (PL 74-271). A number of other laws also provide income replacement for special groups of workers. The UI System provides temporary and partial wage replacement for involuntarily unemployed persons. The aim of the UI System is to provide 50 per cent of a person's lost earnings, but on the average, it falls short of this objective with recipients receiving closer to 35 per cent of their lost earnings.

Funds for Unemployment Insurance are derived from federal and state employer payroll taxes. In three states, employee contributions are deducted from earnings, as well. The rate of taxation allows for the accumulation of reserve funds for periods of high unemployment. The employer payroll tax provides an economic incentive to employers to retain employees during business downturns, but it also creates a group whose interests are served by restrictive eligibility standards and low benefit payments. When employers can prove misconduct as a cause for discharge, employees are ineligible for UI benefits. Employers may receive a deduction in their rate of payment based upon low levels of unemployment claims among their workers. The employers' average rate of contribution has generally increased over time. Between 1970 and 1975, the rate was below 2.0 per cent of taxable payroll. From 1976 to 1983 the rate of contribution ranged from 2.4 per cent to 2.8 per cent of payroll. In 1983 and 1984, the payroll contribution exceeded 3.0 per cent of an average employer's taxable payroll. In 1986 the rate was 2.8 per cent.

The states are responsible for administering the UI program, although the federal government issues policy guidelines and reviews state UI laws for conformity with federal requirements. Programs vary widely from state to state; the common duration of coverage is 26 weeks. The normal duration of benefits is substantially shorter than is typically found in other OECD countries. It is half the duration allowed in West Germany and 60 per cent of the duration of coverage found in Sweden. Under the Employment Security Act Amendments of 1970, the requirements for state UI systems were strengthened.

In 1970, $3.8 billion were paid in state UI benefits. Payments equaled $11.8 billion in 1975, but drifted around $8 billion during the remainder of the decade. However, from 1980 onward total payments under the UI system have exceeded $10 billion in every year, peaking at $20.4 billion in 1982. During that recessionary period, about four million persons were served weekly with an average payment that represented about 36 per cent of a worker's previous wage. This level of compensation has fluctuated very slightly over time. The income replacement rate in the United States is substantially lower than that offered in other OECD countries. By 1986, the annual number of beneficiaries had declined to 8.3 million and total payments equaled $15.4 billion. Information regarding payments and beneficiaries is reported in Table 2.1.

Unemployment insurance is provided through three distinct programs. The majority of payments are made from the regular state unemployment insurance program which is funded by employer payroll taxes; extended payments are shared by the state and federal governments; temporary payments of unemployment insurance benefits are paid with funds from the federal government according to special legislation, such as the Federal Supplemental Compensation Act which is no longer in effect and the Trade Adjustment Assistance Act which continues to operate. Workers in some industries, including steel and auto, are eligible for Supplemental Unemployment Benefits (SUB) which they have secured through the collective bargaining process.

When demands for unemployment benefits within a state exceed available funds, the states may receive a loan from the federal government that must be repaid within a specified period or the state is subject to a penalty tax. In recent years, the Congress has been more strict in the amount of time available to the states for repayment and the granting of deferrals of payments. This, in turn, may put pressure on the states to become more parsimonious in the granting of unemployment insurance benefits.[6]

A list of special federal programs has been enacted to provide unemployment insurance and wage subsidies for workers in transportation industries, particularly railroads. The practice was established with the passage of the Railroad Unemployment Insurance Act of 1938 and the 1940 amendments to the Interstate Commerce Act of 1887.

The Railroad Unemployment Insurance fund, while not as large as the Unemployment Insurance fund, is a sizable program. In the current decade, payments under the Railroad Unemployment Insurance fund peaked in 1982 at $339 million. For the succeeding years, costs have declined to levels observed before the 1981-1982 recession. The data are reported in Table 2.3 along with other income transfers.

Concern for railworkers displaced as a result of federal transportation programs led to the inclusion of provisions for wage subsidies, income replacement and severance pay in the Urban Mass Transportation Act of 1964 (Public Law 89-365) and similar subsequent legislation including the High Speed Ground Transportation Act of 1965 (PL 89-220), the Rail Passenger Services Act of 1970 (PL 91-518), and the Regional Rail Reorganization Act of 1973 (PL 93-236). However, of these three, only the latter has involved significant costs. In the same vein, workers affected by federal

TABLE 2.1

State Unemployment Insurance Fund, 1970 to 1986

Year	Benificiaries (1000s Yearly)	Benefits % of Total Weekly Earnings	Regular Benefits Paid (Billions)	Extended Benefits Paid (Billions)	Average Employer Contribution as % of Taxable Payroll
1970	6402.	36	3.8	—	1.3
1971	6540.	35	5.0	.66	1.5
1972	5704.	36	4.5	.48	1.7
1973	5329.	35	4.0	.14	2.0
1974	7730.	36	6.0	.54	2.0
1975	11160.	36	11.8	2.49	1.9
1976	8560.	36	9.0	2.30	2.6
1977	7985.	35	8.3	1.76	2.8
1978	7565.	35	7.7	.69	2.8
1979	8074.	35	8.9	.24	2.7
1980	9992.	36	13.8	1.76	2.5
1981	9399.	35	13.3	1.36	2.4
1982	11648.	36	20.4	2.46	2.5
1983	8907.	36	17.8	.18	2.8
1984	7743.	35	12.6	.04	3.2
1985	8365.	35	14.0	.07	3.1
1986	8322.	36	15.4	.15	2.8

Source: U.S. Department of Labor, Employment and Training Division, Unemployment Insurance Financial Data, 1983 and supplemental program letters, and unpublished data.

policy to deinstitutionalize delinquent juveniles were provided income insurance (PL 93-415). Finally, workers who lose their job as a result of a major disaster can receive benefits equal to their state's normal unemployment insurance rates for a maximum of one year (PL 93-200).

Under the Trade Act of 1974 (PL 93-610), a special program was established to provide unemployment insurance to persons whose occupations or industries were affected by U.S. trade policy. The Trade Adjustment Assistance Program provides unemployment insurance benefits to displaced workers after the regular UI benefit period has been exhausted. Workers in industries decimated by imported goods such as apparel, footwear, steel, electronics, and automobiles are among those receiving compensation for lost work. The maximum length of benefits is a total of 52 weeks within a two-year period, but workers over 60 years of age or who are in training may receive benefits for a total of 78 weeks within a three-year period. Similarly, amendments to the National Park Act (Public Law 95-250) enacted in 1978 provided full income replacement through 1984 for laid-off federal workers who had been engaged in harvesting redwood timber in California. The Redwood Employee Protection Program became the vehicle through which federal employees receive unemployment benefits and relief.

Table 2.2 provides information regarding the total level of unemployment insurance payments between 1970 and 1986. These payments include regular state unemployment insurance, extended unemployment insurance paid under federal and state authoritities, and temporary benefit programs under various federal programs. Payments peaked as a result of the 1981-1982 recession at $25.5 billion in 1983. Since 1974, payments exceeded ten billion dollars in all but two years (1978 and 1979).

Unemployment insurance payments did not equal or exceed 1 per cent of the U.S. Gross National Product (GNP) during the period between 1970 and 1985, although in 1975 the proportion was just short of 1 per cent at .99. During the most recent periods of high unemployment, payments represented about .73 per cent of GNP. Since 1983 the rate of payment as a proportion of GNP has declined reaching .38 per cent of the cyclically adjusted rate of GNP in 1985. Figure 2.A illustrates this relationship.

During the 1980s, changes in the legislation providing both regular and extended benefits have occurred that reduce overall benefit payments and restrict the rules for benefit eligibility. In 1981, the Omnibus Budget Reconciliation Act (OBRA) modified the Extended Benefits program by increasing the proportion of a state's work force that must be unemployed in order to trigger the distribution of extended benefits and by eliminating the national unemployment rate as a threshold for all states to offer extended payments. In response the 1981-1982 recession which occurred shortly after the passage of OBRA, the temporary Federal Supplemental Compensation Act was passed, but this buffer was phased-out after March 1985.

2.2 Other Instruments for Income Transfer

Income replacement and wage subsidies are available to workers through other social programs. Two of these, the Veterans' Pension Fund and Workers' Compensation have federal outlays at about the same level as the combined unemployment insurance programs. All three of these programs made cash payments of at least 14 billion dollars in 1985, as

TABLE 2.2

Unemployment Insurance Benefits as a Proportion of GNP, 1970-1986

	Total Benefits[a] Paid (Millions)	Percentage of GNP[b]
1970	3811.	.37
1971	5582.	.50
1972	5454.	.45
1973	4188.	.32
1974	6570.	.44
1975	16548.	.99
1976	14280.	.78
1977	11533.	.58
1978	8162.	.39
1979	9100.	.37
1980	15331.	.56
1981	15087.	.49
1982	24592.	.74
1983	25565.	.72
1984	15374.	.41
1985	14970.	.38
1986[c]	15547.	.37

[a]Total benefits include regular, extended and temporary benefits paid with state and federal funds.
[b]GNP is adjusted for cyclical variation.
[c]Estimates derived from U.S. Department of Labor, Bureau of Labor Statistics, *Employment and Training Handbook*.
Source: For 1970-1985: U.S. Congress, House, Testimony of Wayne Vroman of the Urban Institute, Committee on Government Operations, *Changes in the Unemployment Insurance Program*, 22 May 1986.

reported in Table 2.3. Temporary Disability Benefits amounted to substantially less in total payments, but still represented a sizable sum.

2.3 Job Placement Services

The main government instrument for employment placement in the United States is the U.S. Employment Service (USES) which was established in 1932. The USES provides assistance to the states which are responsible

12

FIGURE 2.A UI Benefit Payments
as Percentage of GNP: 1970-1986

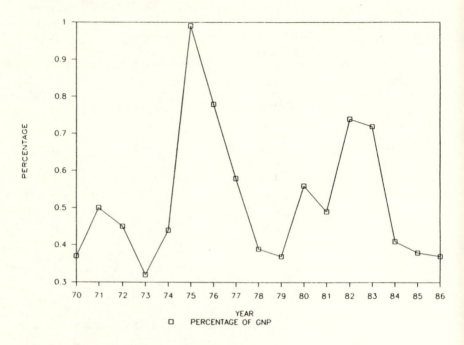

Source: Computed from data reported in Table 2.2.

for establishing and maintaining job placement services and counseling to job seekers. These local offices provide referrals of eligible candidates for vacant position in business and government. Funds for service activities are derived from the Unemployment Trust Fund which is funded through payroll taxes levied against employers by state and federal governments and from other federal employment programs that include a mandate for placement. Service delivery is provided by the states through a nationwide network of local employment service offices which are also responsible for the allocation of public unemployment insurance and for administering various special employment service programs.

Unlike its counterparts in Sweden and West Germany, the public employment service in the U.S. operates in a highly competitive job placement market, with relatively little authority or bureaucratic autonomy and limited resources. The USES is presently attached to the U.S. Department

TABLE 2.3

Public Income Maintenance Programs Cash Benefit Payments in Millions of Current Dollars, 1970-1986

Year	Total in Millions	Veterans Benefits	Unemployment State	Unemployment RR^a	Temporary Disability State	Temporary Disability RR^a	Workers' Compen.	Public Ass't.
1970	60474	5480	4184	38.7	644.6	56.2	1981	4864.4
1975	138598	7668	18188	89.5	902.4	47.6	4568	9288.5
1980	227977	11358	18756	176.1	1299.8	63.2	9632	12144.4
1981	241037	12477	13538	207.2	1525.0	58.4	10596	13188.2
1982	282977	13315	20735	338.7	1567.9	55.6	11403	13030.4
1983	298856	13681	18904	339.1	1580.2	50.1	12183	13891.8
1984	307639	13832	13496	152.9	1584.1	42.0	13265	14581.9
1985	328363	14172	14639	134.3	1900.0	47.3	15170	15276.1
1986	--------	14172	15988	144.7	----	80.1	15977	16125.9

^{a}RR = Railroad Unemployment Insurance.
Source: Social Security Bulletin, 51(February 1988): 42.

of Labor. At the state level, the organizational status of employment service agencies varies; some are independent authorities, others are divisions of a state's department of labor.

In placement activities, the USES competes with private employment agencies and college placement offices which locate jobs for executive, professional, technical and clerical personnel. In the area of trades and crafts jobs, trade unions compete with the USES for jobs and applicants. In all occupational categories government civil service personnel offices are an alternative instrument for job seekers to secure work.

The methods used by job seekers reflect the popularity of different search techniques among unemployed workers. Information on methods used is given in Table 2.4. On the average, the unemployed use slightly more than one method to locate work. The great majority apply directly to a particular employer. It also happens that workers respond to advertised openings or advertise their own services. In 1970, about one-third of all unemployed job seekers applied to the US Employment Service, but the rate of application has been closer to one-fourth of job seekers more recently. With respect to use of USES services, members of racial minorities are somewhat more likely to use the service than white workers.[7]

TABLE 2.4

Uunemployed Job Seekers by Methods Used and Race—Monthly Data,
June 1982-1986

Year/ Race	Total 1000s	Employment Services		Employer				Average Methods
		Public %	Private %	Directly %	Ads %	Friends %	Other %	
1986								
White	5462	23.0	6.3	74.8	35.9	17.3	5.2	1.59
Other	1914	31.5	5.4	74.6	27.1	17.6	3.2	1.55
1985								
White	5518	23.4	5.3	77.3	33.8	18.2	5.1	1.63
Other	1750	30.9	5.7	75.5	31.4	17.9	3.6	1.65
1984								
White	6319	22.5	5.8	77.1	35.1	19.9	4.8	1.65
Other	2009	31.9	5.6	72.6	19.1	28.9	4.4	1.62
1983								
White	8598	22.8	5.2	79.7	34.5	17.0	5.3	1.65
Other	2599	27.0	5.1	79.6	14.2	26.2	4.1	1.56
1982								
White	8299	21.4	6.7	78.0	36.0	16.4	4.3	1.63
Other	2587	30.9	6.2	77.3	27.1	15.3	4.6	1.61

Source: *Employment and Earnings*, June 1982-1986.

A beneficiary of unemployment insurance generally must demonstrate specific efforts to obtain a job such as use of a state employment service as a condition for continued receipt of unemployment insurance benefits. Among persons who were unemployed for four weeks or more, there is an apparent greater likelihood for recipients of unemployment insurance to take advantage of the placement services of the USES than there is for persons who are non-recipients. Of the various possible methods for job search, no other method is as sharply related to receipt of UI benefits. About 73 per cent of UI recipients turned to the USES compared to about 50 per cent of non-recipients. Men were more likely to use the US Employment Service than women regardless of benefit status.[8]

Within the limitations of its penetration of the market, the USES has had a record of filling a large portion of the registered job openings, but during the current decade the ratio of placements to registered job openings, the internal placement rate, was about 50 per cent. These figures are presented in Table 2.5. When an indicator of the total volume of job openings in the market (such as the number of new hires per year) is used, the performance of the USES also appears to decline over time, and its performance level looks substantially weaker.

This external placement rate, or the proportion of USES placements to the number of new hires in the market, has been estimated at 10.2 per cent in 1975 and 5.7 per cent in 1982. These ratios are less than half the external placement rates observed in West Germany; however, the internal placement record of the USES does not appear to differ greatly from that of its West German counterpart.[9] When performance is measured in terms of service to clients, or interviews, the record of the USES again appears to be in decline. The statistical information is recorded in Table 2.5.

2.4 Relocation Allowances

The United States uses a number of different approaches to encourage geographic mobility among workers. In many cases, modest allowances for relocation are provided to workers who meet particular criteria such as employment in an area affected by industry-wide changes or trade policies. Taxpaying Americans are also eligible for partial reimbursement of costs for job seeking and job-related relocation and for temporary living expenses while working at a site away from home. These reimbursements are received after the fact as a deduction from individual income tax obligations to the federal government. The precedence for relocation allowances can be traced back to the Interstate Commerce Act of 1887 which pertains to employees affected by mergers or consolidations within the railroad industry. Similarly, persons affected by consolidations or mergers within the communication industry could receive moving and relocation allowances under the Federal Communications Act of 1943.

During the 1970s, allowances for relocation expenses were included in several pieces of legislation. These funds are typically administered by the state employment security offices. The Regional Rail Reorganization Act of 1973, which includes assistance for losses incurred in the sale of a house as well as relocation allowances, applies to workers affected by railroad reorganizations. The Trade Act of 1974, which applies to workers adversely affected by removal of tariffs on certain imported goods, covers up to 90 per cent of moving expenses and costs for job search. Additionally, a cash allowance limited to $800 is available for related relocation expenses. The maximum allowance in 1985 was $1,600.[10] Federal outlays for job search and relocation activities under the Trade Adjustment Act reached 4.5 million dollars in 1984; thereafter outlays were combined with the retraining outlays.

Workers who are unemployed as a result of a declared national disaster may receive relocation expenses and assistance for housing payments and

TABLE 2.5

Activities and Performance of the U.S. Employment Service, 1975 through 1986

Year	Internal Placement Rate[a]	Job Openings Received 1000s	Place-ments 1000s[b]	Inter-views 1000s	Appli-cations 1000s[c]
1975	40	7889	3,138	1644	18,513
1976	44	7668	3,367	1562	20.098
1977	49	8396	4,137	1654	21,161
1978	48	9534	4,623	1718	20,518
1979	48	9477	4,537	1791	20,090
1980	50	8122	4,088	1776	21,626
1981	49	7548	3,728	1069	21,718
1982	49	6150	3,026	694	19,563
1983	49	6494	3,214	660	20,002
1984	68	5144	3,480	621	20,042
1985	49	6950	3,430	641	19,912
1986	52	6968	3,657	641	19,219

[a]Internal placement rate is the number of employment service placements divided by the number of vacancies reported to the employment service. (Janoski, 1983).
[b]Includes agricultural placements.
[c]Figures include all intake, representing multiple applications by one individual. Data for single applicants not available.
Source: Published and unpublished data, U.S. Department of Labor, Employment and Training Administration.

repairs under the Disaster Relief Act of 1974. Under the 1978 Amendments to the Comprehensive Employment and Training Act, funds for relocation loans and grants as well as allowances for job search assistance were available to unemployed workers residing in areas of high unemployment with little possibility for securing employment in their current place of residence.[11] Finally, under Title III of the Job Training Partnership Act of 1982, eligible dislocated workers may receive partial compensation for relocation costs.

2.5 Expenditures for Training and Job Creation Measures

In the current period, federal allocations for training and job creation measures have declined substantially from previous decades. At present, the most important federal program is the Job Training Partnership (JTPA). JTPA includes eight specific appropriations categories, the largest of which is Training for Economically Disadvantaged persons (Title II, Part A), as shown in Table 2.6. The second area by funding level is the Summer Youth Employment and Training Program (Title II, Part B), which received 624 million dollars in the summer of 1987. By funding level the Assistance for Dislocated workers (Title III) which received 72 million dollars in program

TABLE 2.6

Allocations and Expenditures Under JTPA, 1984-1986

	Title IIA Economically Disadvantaged	Title III Dislocated Workers	Title IIB Summer Youth Employment
Period	Millions of Dollars	Millions of Dollars	Millions of Dollars
FY 1984			
Allotments	1,417	94	811
Total Available	1,542	200	812
Expenditures	1,027	76	701
Expenditure Rate %	67	39	86
FY 1984			
Allotments	1,891	167	810
Total Available	2,406	340	922
Expenditures	1,691	161	788
Expenditure Rate %	70	47	85
PY 1985			
Allotments	1,890	167	711
Total Available	2,605	401	846
Expenditures	1,691	190	764
Expenditure Rate %	72	47	90
PY 1986			
Allotments	1,787	72	624
Total Available	2,525	307	706
Expenditures	1,896	192	617
Expenditure Rate %	75	63	87

Source: Unpublished data, U. S. Department of Labor. Data exclude Virgin Islands and Pacific Island territories.

year 1986 was the fourth largest target program, but the total available funds including carry-overs from preceding years was 307 million. The Job Corps program (Title IV) represents less than 2 per cent of the total appropriation. The 1987 level for this program was $646.8 million. The remaining programs including North Americans, National Activities, Management Workers, and Veterans received substantially less funds.

It is noteworthy that the expenditure patterns for JTPA programs involve considerable carry-over of resources from year to year, particularly in the cases of Title IIA, Economically Disadvantaged, and Title III, the Dislocated Workers Program, as can be seen in Table 2.6. For the former, the expenditure rate ranged from 67 per cent of available funds in transition year 1984 to 75 per cent in program year 1986. For Dislocated Workers, expenditures ranged from only 39 per cent to 63 per cent of available resources for the same periods. Utilization of available funds was much greater for Title IIB, Summer Youth program, which fluctuated around 86 per cent of available monies. For all programs the rate of expenditure increases over time.

In 1984, the Perkins Vocational Education Act was passed. It authorized $63 million in 1985 for training services to single parents and displaced homemakers. In 1986 (FY) allocations for the Perkins Act fell by about 4.5 per cent. Some states have combined their own funds with appropriations from the Perkins Act and the JTPA in order to meet training needs of women.

Similarly, appropriations for the WIN (work incentives) program have declined over the 1980s and so have the number of new program registrants. In 1981, $365 million were approved for this program with an estimated welfare cost savings of $760 million derived from 169,000 employed welfare recipients. For 1986 the program authorizations were estimated at $283 million.[12]

The extent to which the United States invests in its human resources is difficult to assess in that federal outlays for training and employment are found in several different federal agencies and distinctions between training measures and job creation expenditures are not consistently available. Researchers produce different results in estimating federal outlays for employment and training that may indicate lower or higher effort as computed by the proportion of GNP spent on employment policies. The U.S. Budget provides information that demonstrates the importance of federal departments in addition to the Department of Labor in the overall expenditure of funds for employment related activities.

Table 2.7 shows that employment related allocations for the U.S. Department of Education have historically mirrored those of the Department of Labor. Sizable sums are also found in the budgets of the Veterans

TABLE 2.7

Federal Outlays for Training and Employment by Year,
in Four Federal Agencies and Departments

	Fiscal Years 1970-1987 in Billions of dollars					
	Labor	Education	Veterans	HHS[a]	SUM	% of GNP
1970	1.6	1.6	1.0	.6	4.8	.5
1971	2.0	2.0	1.6	.7	6.3	.6
1972	2.9	2.9	2.0	.7	8.5	.7
1973	3.2	3.3	2.8	.8	10.1	.8
1974	2.9	2.9	3.2	.8	9.8	.7
1975	4.1	4.1	4.6	.8	13.6	.9
1976[b]	6.3	8.3	6.1	1.2	21.9	1.0
1977	1.9	6.9	3.7	1.0	13.5	.7
1978	6.9	10.8	3.4	.9	22.0	1.0
1979	10.8	10.8	2.8	.6	25.0	1.0
1980	10.3	10.3	2.3	.7	23.6	.9
1981	9.2	9.2	2.3	.8	21.5	.7
1982	5.5	5.5	1.9	.7	13.6	.4
1983	5.3	4.6	1.6	.6	12.1	.3
1984	4.6	5.0	1.4	.4	11.4	.3
1985	5.0	5.3	1.1	.5	11.9	.3
1986	5.2	5.0	.5	.5	11.2	.3
1987[c]	5.0	5.0	.4	.4	10.8	.2

[a](HHS = Health and Human Services)
[b]1976 includes the transitional quarter between the previous and current defini-
tions of the fiscal year. Percentage of GNP is based on GNP levels from the U.S.
Department of Commerce, Bureau of Economic Analysis.
[c]Data for 1987 are estimates.
Source: U.S. Department of Commerce, Bureau of the Census, Statistical Abstract of
the U.S., 1987, Table 480.

Administration and the Department of Health and Human Services. For all
programs, allocations in actual dollars have declined during the latter part
of the 1980s. The total allocations for these four organizations was $21.5
billion in 1981 as compared with $10.8 billion in 1987. According to the
Congressional Quarterly, for Labor and Education, the 1988 congressional
authorizations are $3.8 and $2.6 billion respectively, which is $3.6 billion
less than the combined allocation for these departments in 1987. This is not

an inclusive list of allocations to federal agencies and departments. Not shown, for example, are allocations to the Departments of Agriculture and Interior which received $12 million and $9.5 million respectively in 1987 for employment related activities.[13]

Federal outlays for employment related activities in the U.S. represent a very small portion of the Gross National Product (GNP). As a percentage of GNP, the U.S. expenditure on employment related activities in these four organizations exceeded 1 per cent in only three of the last 17 years, as can be seen in Table 2.7. While there was a clear upward trend in outlays during the 1970s, the proportion declined during the 1980s. The allotments from 1983 onward have been less than .4 per cent and in the last year for which data are available, 1987, the level was only .2 per cent of GNP. In contrast, the level of expenditure in West Germany and Sweden increased during the same period.[14] These estimates of U.S. effort are higher than those produced by Janoski who excluded programs for youth and veterans from his calculation of federal allocations for employment and training programs.[15]

It is noteworthy that the level of outlays in these four major program areas does not appear to increase in response to the level of unemployment. In fact, the general pattern of association between outlays for employment related activities and unemployment is inverse as can be seen in Figure 2.B. That is, as unemployment increases, less money is directed by the Congress toward unemployment activities in the four organizations. This is in stark contrast to the patterns found in Sweden and West Germany where appropriations for employment measures are positively associated with the level of unemployment. Moreover, it is important to observe that the U.S. figures represent outlays of funds rather than expenditures. The latter might be significantly less than the amount of money available. Thus Figure 2.B might overestimate the amount of effort expended to address employment problems.

2.6 Summary

In this chapter information pertaining to labor market policy measures and expenditures has been presented. Employment policy in the United States has been characterized as compensatory in nature, providing income replacement, remedial training, and temporary employment to persons who meet certain eligibility criteria.

Income replacement through unemployment insurance is a key component of U.S. labor market policy, representing close to 1 per cent of GNP during recessionary periods but never exceeding that amount. Job search assistance is provided by the U.S. Employment Service through a network

FIGURE 2.B Outlays for Training and Employment
in Four Federal Organizations: 1970-1987

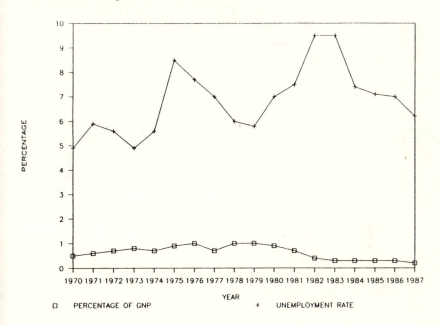

Source: See Table 2.7.

of local state government operated offices. About half of all jobs filed with the USES are filled. Relocation allowances are offered to unemployed workers in specific categories.

There is no centralized administration of federally-sponsored training programs. Outlays for four federal organizations between 1970 and 1987 were presented as an indicator of government expenditures for training. In 1986 and 1987 a total of about $11 billion was allocated to the Departments of Labor, Education and Health and Human Services and to the Veterans Administration for training and employment programs. This amounted to .3 per cent of the 1986 GNP. The proportion of Gross National Product allocated to training and employment peaked in the late 1970s at 1 per cent but has steadily declined since then.

In the next chapter information pertaining to changes in the supply of and demand for labor is presented. Statistics regarding the pattern of labor force participation and shifts in the structure of employment provide insight into the American labor market strategy of creating special programs that target specific population groups. A pattern of growth in both the supply of labor and the rate of labor force participation is evident in the U.S. although declines in the rate of labor force activity are apparent for some groups of workers, particularly those who have passed their prime work years.

3
Changing Trends in
Labor Supply and Demand

In this section, patterns in the supply and demand for labor will be presented for the period between 1970 and 1987. A characteristic of the U.S. labor market is its flexibility, but in recent years that feature has undergone considerable scrutiny.

3.1 Labor Market Supply Factors

The United States has historically had an expanding labor force, but forecasters predict a shortage of labor in the twenty-first century in conjunction with a decline in population growth. In 1987 the U.S. work force included 121.6 million workers. Data regarding the employment status of the non-institutional population is provided in Table 3.1. About 66 per cent of the total non-institutional population 16 years of age and older participates in the work force. This reflects a small increase in the rate of labor force participation over the last decade. In 1960 about 60 per cent of the population was in the work force. The participation rate in 1987 was about 66 per cent. The total work force is composed of non-employees and members of the armed forces. Unemployment levels this decade ranged from 9.5 per cent in 1982 and 1983 to 5.5 per cent in 1988. The civilian unemployment rate has steadily declined since 1983.

The size of the U.S. population has steadily increased, with a growth rate of 15.6 per cent or 26 million workers over the last decade. Expansion of the population, however, is not expected to continue into the next century. Forecasters predict that the population will peak at about 300 million people and this, in turn, is expected to produce a labor shortage.

TABLE 3.1

Employment Status of the Noninstitutional U.S. Population 16 Years of Age and Older, 1977-1987

Population 1000s (1)		In Labor Force 1000s (2)	% (2/1)	Unemployed 1000s (3)	% (3/2)	Not in Labor Force 1000s (4)	% (4/1)
1977	160,689	100,665	62.6	6,991	6.9	60,025	37.4
1978	163,541	103,882	63.5	6,202	6.0	59,659	36.5
1979	166,460	106,559	64.0	6,137	5.8	59,000	35.4
1980	169,349	108,544	64.1	7,637	7.0	60,806	35.9
1981	171,775	110,315	64.2	8,273	7.5	61,460	35.8
1982	173,939	111,872	64.3	10,678	9.5	62,067	35.7
1983	175,891	113,226	64.4	10,717	9.5	62,665	35.6
1984	178,080	115,241	64.7	8,539	7.4	62,839	35.6
1985	179,912	117,167	65.1	8,312	7.1	62,744	34.9
1986[a]	182,293	119,540	65.6	8,237	6.9	62,752	34.4
1987	184,490	121,602	65.9	7,425	6.1	62,888	34.1

[a]Not strictly comparable with other years.
Source: Employment and Earnings 35(March 1988): 600.

The U.S. Bureau of Labor Statistics predicts that the work force will include 139 million workers in the year 2000. The composition of the future work force is expected to reflect greater labor force participation on the part of minority group members and changes in the age distribution of workers. Fewer workers under 25 years of age and fewer workers over 55 years old are anticipated. With respect to ethnic and racial composition, the Caucasian share of the work force is expected to decline slightly from 86 per cent in 1986 to 84 per cent by the year 2000. Of the racial and ethnic minorities, the fastest growth is predicted for Hispanic workers whose share of the labor force is expected to expand from eight million workers to 14 million workers by 2000, which would equal 10 per cent of the projected labor force. Both immigration and fertility patterns are taken into account in this estimate.[16]

Given the difficulties in assessing cross-national variations in unemployment rates, the employment-population ratio, which indicates the proportion of persons employed relative to the working age civilian population, is a useful work force statistic. The U.S. Bureau of Labor Statistics attempts to apply U.S. concepts to other nations for comparative purposes.

It is noteworthy that the U.S. employment-population ratio has improved during the second half of the 1980s. The U.S. rate has consistently lagged behind the employment-population ratio in Sweden, a country which sets a rather high international standard for labor force participation. The Swedish labor force participation rate exceeded .64 over the last ten years. In comparison, the proportion of the working age population involved in the labor force in West Germany has declined in recent years with a ratio of less than .50 since 1982, according to the U.S. Bureau of Labor Statistics. Table 3.2 presents the employment population ratios for the three countries.

3.2 Demographic Factors Affecting Labor Pool

Expansion of the labor supply is attributable to demographic factors that are not unique to the United States. As was the case in many other nations, the U.S. population experienced a sharp increase as a result of the size of the post World War II birth cohort. Second, a dramatic increase in the rate of female labor force participation has contributed to the size of the work force. At the same time, lower fertility rates among adult females and fewer interruptions in their working lives have increased the number of persons in the work force at a given time. A contemporary factor of particular importance is the northward immigration of Hispanic people from South and Central America into the United States.

TABLE 3.2

Employment-Population Ratios[a] in Three Countries Using U.S. Concepts

	1977	1980	1981	1982	1983	1984	1985	1986
United States	.579	.592	.590	.578	.579	.595	.601	.607
Sweden	.648	.656	.651	.647	.644	.645	.650	.654
W. Germany	.516	.517	.508	.496	.486	.485	.487	.491

[a]Employment as a proportion of the civilian working-age population.
Source: Monthly Labor Review 111(January 1988): 116.

The United States has experienced steady growth in the size of its labor force since World War II. Between 1968 and 1973, a growth rate of 2.2 per cent occurred when the large post-war birth cohort began to enter the labor market. Continued growth at an annual rate of 2.6 per cent occurred over the next six years (1973-1979) as women accelerated their rate of labor force participation. In absolute terms, an increase of 28.7 million workers occurred in the 15 years between 1970 and 1985. The rate of growth in the U.S. labor force clearly exceeds the growth rate in West Germany and Sweden. Germany saw considerably less labor force expansion, and the U.S. rate doubled that in Sweden in each time period. In comparison to the average annual growth rate for all OECD countries, the U.S. exceeded the mean rate of growth by 1.4 per cent from 1979 to 1986. According to projections reported by the OECD, the U.S. labor force is expected to continue to expand through 1995 at an annual average rate of 1.0 per cent. For the same period, a commensurate work force decline is estimated for West Germany and a growth rate between .5 and .7 per cent is projected for Sweden. Average annual growth rates for the three nations are given in Table 3.3.

TABLE 3.3

Average Annual Growth Rate of National Labor Forces for Selected Time Periods

	1968-73	1973-79	1979-86
United States	2.2	2.6	1.6
Sweden	.8	1.2	.6[a]
West Germany	.7	-.2	.6
Total OECD	1.3	1.4	1.2 estimates

[a](1979 to 1985)
Source: OECD, Employment Outlook, September 1987, 54.

This growth in the U.S. population translates into changes in the age composition of the work force. In 1960, 23 per cent of the civilian work force was between 35 and 44 years of age, 21 per cent was between 25 and 34 years, and 10 per cent was between 20 and 24 years. Changes in these proportions as a result of the large post World War II birth cohort became apparent in the mid-1970s. In 1975, 18 per cent of the work force was in the prime age category of 35-44 years. This is about 5 per cent less than the 1960 level. But from 1980 onward, the change in work force composition by age became more pronounced. In 1980, 19 per cent of the workers were between 35-44 years and 27 per cent were in the younger 25-34 age category. This group included 29.4 per cent of the work force in 1987. In 1987, the 35-44-year-olds represented 24 per cent of the work force, while the older 45-54-year-old group declined from 21 per cent in 1960, to 15.6 per cent in 1987. Table 3.4 reports the age composition of the work force from 1960 to 1987.

TABLE 3.4

Age Composition of the U.S. Work Force, Selected Years 1960-1987

	16-19 years	20-24 years	25-34 years	35-44 years	45-54 years	55+ years
1960	7.0	9.6	20.7	23.4	21.3	18.1
1965	7.9	11.1	19.1	22.6	21.2	18.1
1970	8.8	12.8	20.6	19.9	20.5	17.5
1975	9.5	14.7	24.4	18.0	18.2	15.3
1980	8.8	14.9	27.3	19.1	15.8	14.1
1985	6.8	13.6	29.1	22.6	15.0	12.9
1986	5.9	12.6	29.4	23.6	15.5	13.1
1987	5.9	12.0	29.4	24.2	15.6	12.9

Sources: U.S. Department of Commerce, Bureau of the Census, Statistical Abstract of the U.S., 1987, Table 640; Employment and Earnings 35(January 1988): Table 19.

Immigration, which has been principally accomplished through a high rate of growth among the Hispanic population, has been a significant factor in the size of the U.S. labor supply in recent decades. It is not only an increased number of Hispanics in the population but also an apparent greater propensity to work outside the home among Hispanic women which contribute to work force growth. Between 1983 and 1987 an increase of 21 per cent of total U.S. employment growth is attributable to Hispanic workers.[17] These increases have offset a subtle pattern of declining labor force participation among men and a sharper rate of decline among senior workers. These trends will be examined more closely.

3.3 Participation Rates Affecting Labor Pool

As in other countries, one of the most important factors affecting the supply of labor is the rate of labor force participation among women. Women are responsible for 60 per cent of the growth in the work force between 1970-1985. By 1987, 56 per cent of all American women over 16 years of age were members of the work force. Participation rates are given in Table 3.5. The rate of participation among American women is somewhat higher than that observed for most European women including Germans but lower than the Swedish female participation rate.[18] The flow of women into the labor market was particularly high during the 1970s when more than 11 million entered or re-entered the work force. Between 1950 and 1987 the proportion of women 16 years of age and over in the work force increased by 23 per cent. During the 1980s more than half of all women have worked outside the home and women's share of the total U.S. labor force now equals 44 per cent. The unprecedented entrance of women into the American work force has made significant changes in the supply and utilization of human resources.

Certain demographic factors are related to female labor force participation. A large portion of the influx into the labor market is attributable to women between 20 and 44 years of age. Whereas about 44 per cent of this group was in the work force in 1965, the rate of participation climbed to 71 per cent within 20 years. Almost three-fourths of women in this age group are in the work force today. Older women have also increased their rate of employment, but not as dramatically. As shown in Figure 3.A from 1965 to 1985, the participation rate for women between 45 and 54 years of age rose from 51 per cent to 65 per cent, an increase of 14 percentage points. For those over 55 years of age there was no significant change. While female labor force participation rates are generally higher (61 per cent) for women who maintain a family on their own than for women living with a husband (55 per cent), the participation rates for women with and without small children (under six years) have recently equalized at about 55 per cent. As in other countries, contemporary working-age women are demonstrating an inclination to delay or forego childbearing and have produced fewer children than their mothers' generation. At the same time, American women with small children tend to re-enter the work force more quickly.[19]

In contrast, among American men a pattern of declining work force participation is evident, although the rate of decline is relatively slow. From 1950 to 1987, the male labor force participation rate declined from 86 per cent to 76 per cent, a change of 10 per cent. Male employment participation rates in the U.S. are almost as high as those observed in Sweden.[20] While prime working age males have not significantly changed their rate of labor force participation, among married men between 45 and 64 years of age, participation rates declined by 11 per cent between 1960 and 1986. Racial differences are apparent among men with a higher rate of decline in labor force participation among non-white males. For single men, a change of 13 percentage points is estimated. Among American men between 55 and 64 years of age exit from the work force is becoming increasingly popular. A 15 per cent decline in their rate of participation occurred between 1970 and 1987.[21] Figure 3.B displays male participation patterns by age which are given in Table 3.5.

Increased rates of labor force participation are apparent for other demographic groups, including young persons between 16 and 24 years of age. For all young adults participation increased from 60 per cent in 1970 to 68 per cent of the youth population in 1985. Young workers represent one-fifth of the U.S. labor force, but their unemployment level is relatively high with respect to both the overall U.S. labor force and to unemployment rates for youth in West Germany and Sweden.

About 7 per cent of the U.S. work force in 1987 was Hispanic. Almost 11 per cent of U.S. workers are black males. Historically, black women have had higher participation rates than white females, but this pattern leveled off during the 1970s as more white women entered the work force. Similarly, Hispanic females have increased their rate of labor force participation. In 1987, 55.7 per cent of Hispanic women worked outside the home.

3.4 Linkage between Education and Labor Force Participation

Education is a factor affecting the pattern of labor force participation as well as an indicator of the quality of the labor pool. The U.S. has participated in a global trend toward higher average years of schooling and broader participation in education. In 1960 the mean years of schooling was 10.6. By 1985 that level had reached 12.6 years. By 1987, one-fourth of the U.S. labor force held a college degree. There was an increase in the proportion of white, black, and Hispanic workers who had completed some college level schooling between 1975 and 1985 and there was a substantial decline in the proportion of blacks who dropped out of school over the same ten-year period. Unemployment rates are lowest for the most educated persons. While college graduates had an unemployment rate of 2.5 per cent in March 1987, high school graduates were unemployed at a rate of 6.3 per cent and dropouts suffered a rate of 11.1 per cent unemployment. The increased share of persons with college degrees in the labor market has apparently reduced the market value of a high school education making those with less than a college education more likely to be affected by cyclical swings in the economy. Moreover, structural changes in the economy do not favor persons with low levels of education. More than 80 per cent of all college graduates are employed in the rapidly growing service sector.[22]

Race is an important factor in interpreting the effects of different levels of education on an individual's employment status, as the data in Table 3.6 report. A general decrease in the level of unemployment by educational level is apparent for both whites and Hispanics. Among blacks and Hispanics, only the highest level of education, four or more years of college (bachelors degree or higher), translates into equal rates of unemployment

**FIGURE 3.A Civilian Female Participation Rates
by Age Group: 1965-1985**

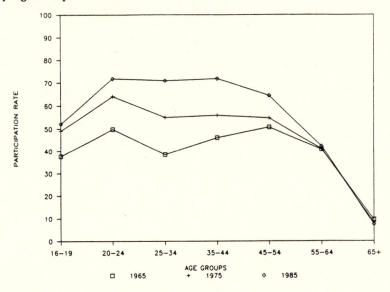

**FIGURE 3.B Civilian Male Participation Rates
by Age Group: 1965-1985**

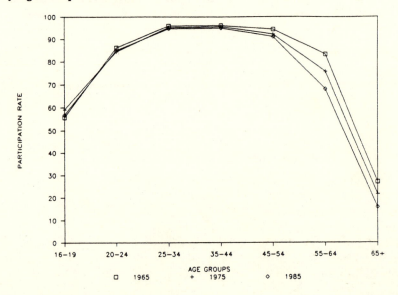

Source: Table 3.5.

TABLE 3.5

Labor Force Participation Rates by Sex and Age, 1965-1987

	16-19	20-24	25-34	Age Group 35-44	45-54	55-64	65+	All
Males								
1965	55.7	86.2	96.0	96.2	94.3	83.2	26.9	80.7
1970	56.1	83.3	96.4	96.9	94.3	83.0	26.8	79.7
1975	59.1	84.5	95.2	95.6	92.1	75.6	21.6	77.9
1980	60.5	85.9	95.2	95.5	91.2	72.1	19.0	77.4
1985	56.8	85.0	94.7	95.0	91.0	67.9	15.8	76.3
1987	56.1	85.2	94.6	94.6	90.7	67.6	16.3	76.2
Females								
1965	37.7	49.7	38.5	45.9	50.5	40.6	9.5	39.3
1970	44.0	57.7	45.0	51.1	54.4	43.0	9.7	43.3
1975	49.1	64.1	54.0	55.8	54.6	40.9	8.2	46.3
1980	52.0	68.9	65.5	65.5	59.9	41.3	8.1	51.5
1985	52.1	71.8	70.9	71.8	64.4	42.0	7.3	54.5
1987	53.3	73.0	72.4	74.5	67.1	42.7	7.4	56.0

Sources: U.S. Department of Commerce, Bureau of Labor Statistics,*U.S. Statistical Abstract*, 1987, Table 198; Data for 1987 computed from *Employment and Earnings* 35(January 1988): Table 3.

with the white population. At the same time, blacks with four or more years of college education display the highest rates of labor force participation in both time periods. Among whites and Hispanics, labor force participation rates for college graduates are equal in both 1977 and 1987.

3.5 Level of Participation

A change in the U.S. labor market is revealed by the proportion of persons working part-time and the number of persons holding temporary jobs. In this section, information regarding these trends is presented in order to provide some insight into the changing dynamics of the U.S. labor market. Taking part-time hours and temporary work into account, about 59 per cent of the U.S. work force is employed full-time year round. Part-time employment is particularly compatible with the growing service industry in that it allows employers to adjust working hours to peak service delivery periods. Expansion of the labor force dictates a diversion from the tradi-

TABLE 3.6

Labor Force Status by Years of School Completed and Race
for March 1977 and 1987

	White 1977 1987	Black 1977 1987	Hispanic 1977 1987
Labor Force *Participation*	% %	% %	% %
• Less than High School	72 78	71 75	67 73
• 4 years of			
High School	71 77	77 78	72 77
• 1-3 yrs. college	76 82	82 84	81 83
• 4 or more yrs college	85 88	91 90	85 88
Unemployment			
• Less than High School	8 10	11 15	11 12
• 4 years of			
High School	5 6	10 12	8 8
• 1-3 yrs. college	4 4	10 8	7 7
• 4 or more yrs college	3 2	3 4	4 3

Source: U.S. Department of Labor, Bureau of Labor Statistics, *News*, 87-415, September 1987.

tional nine to five, five days per week, mode of work. Greater flexibility in the structure and terms of employment make work force participation compatible with the responsibilities and preferences of a larger portion of the population.

Part-time Employment. Part-time employment has not been as popular in the United States as it has been in other countries, but during the current decade, the American work day has become more flexible. In 1987, about 19 per cent of the American civilian labor force worked part-time. This is an increase of four per cent over the 1970 rate. Of new jobs created between 1979 and 1985, a period within which the U.S. recovered from two economic recessions, the number of part-time jobs grew faster than full time jobs. Jobs of less than 35 hours per week composed 30 per cent of all net employment growth. The growing proportion of part-time jobs partly accounts for a downward shift in the profile of weekly earnings over time.

As in other countries, women are more likely to work part-time than men, but the difference is not as sharp in the United States. About 55 per cent of part-timers are female; but only 30 per cent of all working women held part-time jobs in 1986. In 1970, 22 per cent of women worked part-time, and 52 per cent of the part-time labor force was female.

Among teenagers, part-time work is more typical than full-time employment. Two-thirds of the persons between 16 and 19 years of age who were in the work force in 1986 held part-time jobs. Men over 20 years of age generally form less than 20 per cent of the part-time work force; the proportion in 1987 was 25 per cent. The rate was 5.6 per cent lower in 1970. As the data in Table 3.7 indicate, changes in the distribution of part-time employment in the United States have been rather subtle for adults while teenagers form a smaller portion of the part-time work force today.

Youths enrolled in school are much more likely to work part-time than those who have left the educational system. About 80 per cent of working youth enrolled in school worked part-time in 1987. Conversely, only 18 per cent of those out of school and in the work force held part-time jobs.[23]

Involuntary Part-time Employment. Involuntary part-time employment, which involves people who are working part-time for economic reasons, is an indicator of underemployment. The volume of workers in this category varies cyclically with economic condition but the impact of economic conditions in the United States is much greater during periods of

TABLE 3.7

Part-time[a] Employment Status of the U.S. Civilian Work Force, by Sex and Age: 1970 to 1987

	1970	1975	1980	1985	1986	1987
Part-time as Per cent of work force	14.1	14.6	14.6	16.4	17.5	17.7
Total Part-Time in 1000s	11703	13659	15644	16283	20598	21189
Per cent of part-time:						
Males, 20 years and older	19.3	19.0	18.4	19.3	21.8	24.9
Females, 20 years and older	51.9	51.6	53.6	56.3	54.9	54.7
Youth, 16-19 years old	28.8	29.3	28.0	24.4	23.3	20.4

[a]Part-time represents all employment less than 35 hours per week.
Sources: Employment and Earnings, various issues, 18(January 1971) through 35(January 1988).

recession than it is in recovery periods. Workers most likely to have their hours reduced or to take jobs with shorter work weeks because of economic conditions are disproportionately teenagers, blacks, and females.[24] The proportion of persons working part-time who say they would prefer a full-time job increased sharply between 1981 and 1983, a period of cyclical unemployment. While the rate of involuntary part-time workers has declined slowly since then, it has not returned to pre-recessionary 1981 levels.

In 1985, 22 per cent of those working part-time cited economic factors as the reason for working less than 35 hours per week. This amounted to 5.6 million workers, a slight improvement over the preceding years. Of these cases, 3.6 million cases were directly attributed to slack work. Slightly less than one-third of those working part-time for economic reasons reported they were usually employed full-time. As a proportion of the total civilian labor force, involuntary part-timers represented about 4.5 per cent of all workers in 1986 and 1985. Between 1965 and 1980, involuntary part-time work did not exceed four per cent of the civilian work force. Figure 3.C reveals the trends in involuntary part-time employment from 1965 to 1985. In 1987, 27 per cent of those working part-time cited economic reasons and of these 12 per cent specified slack work as the cause. Another 13 per cent said they could only find part-time work. About 5.3 million people were involuntarily working part-time in 1987.[25]

Temporary Employment. Temporary employment, either directly with a particular employer or through an employment placement service, is becoming increasingly popular in the United States. Official statistics are not compiled by the U.S. Departments of Labor or Commerce pertaining to the number of persons in temporary employment arrangements. In the past, temporary employment was not of significant scale in the U.S., but since the last economic recession hiring of full-time temporary employees has expanded. About one million persons work full-time in temporary jobs through the temporary help industry. According to the National Association of Temporary Services, five million people work as temporary employees per year.[26]

The rate of growth in the temporary help industry demands attention. According to government estimates, the temporary work force doubled between 1978 and 1985. Between 1982 and 1983, expansion of temporary jobs accounted for 3 per cent of the total growth in jobs in the U.S. There is no count of persons who individually make temporary work arrangements with an employer. Statistics pertaining to part-time and part-year work are indicative of the trend and self-employment may represent a share of these workers. Growth in the industry is clearly cyclical, reflecting changes in the business cycle. A sharp increase in temporary employment in the late 1970s tapered off with the onset of the 1981-1982 recession. At the peak of the recession, the industry shed 8.4 per cent of its workers.

Temporary jobs are most commonly found in occupations providing administrative and sales support, including clerical work. In fact, the great majority of these jobs are in clerical and administrative support occupations (43.3 per cent). While less than 5 per cent of the temporary work force performs skilled manual labor, when combined with operators, fabricators, repair and crafts workers (who amount to almost 17 per cent of the temporary work force), one in five temporary workers is involved in production. About one in ten temporary jobs is found in service occupations.[27]

This trend toward contingent workers is also apparent in the public sector. In 1985, the U.S. government expanded the authority under which federal agencies could hire temporary workers and increased the duration of temporary appointments to four years. This change led to more than 7,000 additional temporary appointments in one year, an increase of 22.4 per cent in the size of the federal temporary work force. In 1985, there were 42,118 temporary appointments in the U.S. federal civilian work force. The great majority of these positions (66%) involve clerical work.[28]

The degree of reliance upon contingent workers can be interpreted as an indicator of the level of maturity of an economic recovery. A preference for contingent workers reflects uncertainty about future labor needs and an unwillingness to commit permanent positions to additional workers. Instead, employers pursue a short-term hiring strategy which protects them from over-expansion of the labor force by using temporary "discardable" workers. In addition to being able to shed these workers quickly in the event of an economic downturn, management makes little investment in training or incentives to enhance organizational commitment among these workers.

Temporary workers are generally a cheaper source of labor. Many work in a part-time status, others work a full day sporadically. In addition to a lack of job security, in most cases temporary employees receive none of the benefits usually obtained through employment such as health insurance or retirement benefits. This applies to temporary employees in government, as well as those working in the private sector.[29] In that their services are easily terminated during economic downturns, temporary workers insulate the bulk of the work force from cyclical swings in the economy. Given the fact that temporary workers are disproportionately female, young, and black, their disadvantageous employment conditions are concerning.

Despite these disadvantages, temporary employment arrangements meet the work needs and preferences of many people. Those who voluntarily choose temporary terms of employment cite the variety in work

FIGURE 3.C Number of Persons Working Part-time Involuntarily by Major
Reason, Seasonally Adjusted Quarterly Averages, 1965-85

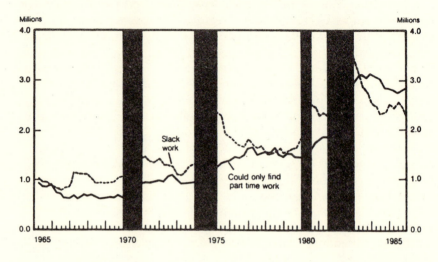

Note: Shaded areas indicate recessions as designated by the National Bureau of
Economic Research

Source: Robert W. Bednarzik, "Involuntary Part-time Work: A Cyclical Analysis," *Monthly Labor Review*, september, 1975: 12-18.

assignments as well as the greater compatibility of work schedules with
personal obligations. Moreover, the temporary help supply industry facilitates entry and re-entry into the job market reducing the costs of job search
and providing references for its employees. Persons in seasonal occupations seek temporary employment during transition periods in their normal
work cycle. Women with family responsibilities are key candidates for jobs
in the temporary help industry in that employment can be adjusted to meet
both daily and cyclical family responsibilities. Persons re-entering the work
force who are unsure of their skills and employability may find a temporary
employment situation preferable to a permanent commitment to a particular employer in that it allows them to "test the market" and facilitates
changes in an unsatisfactory career or job situation.[30]

3.6 Trends in the Demand for Labor

The global trend of an increase in the proportion of total employment
attributable to the service sector is clearly evident in the United States, but

the causes for and implications of this structural shift are less obvious. In this section, information pertaining to the volume and proportion of employment from 1970 to 1986 is presented in order to obtain a clearer view of the nature of the shifts in the demand structure. While the data indicate clear movement away from manufacturing and other production jobs, manufacturing output in the United States continues to represent more than 20 per cent of the Gross National Product. While some analysts predict steady growth in factory output, there is no expectation that employment in goods production will return to previous levels. On the other hand, growth in employment in agriculture, forestry and fishing has been observed and is expected to continue into the future. However, much of this employment is service oriented, involving horticultural and landscaping services. Finally, in the area of primary metals, a continued but slower rate of decline is anticipated.[31] Table 3.8 reports the volume of employment by industry from 1978-1986.

From 1970 to 1987, the number of non-agricultural jobs in the U.S. increased from 70.9 million to 102.1 million as shown in Table 3.9. The great bulk of growth in the number of jobs is attributable to the private service sector (85 million). The service-producing sector (which includes transportation, trade, public utilities, finance, insurance, real estate, health, education, and government) has historically demonstrated steady growth, but an increase in the rate of growth became apparent in the 1960s.

Goods Production. About one-fourth of the 1987 work force was involved in goods production, whereas one-third of the work force was found in that area in 1970. During the same period there was a net growth of 1.3 million jobs in the goods producing sector. Within the goods production sector job losses occurred in manufacturing and this structural change was exacerbated by economic recession. Between 1970 and 1987, 255,000 jobs were lost in manufacturing. Employment in manufacturing declined from 27.3 per cent of the total work force to 18.7 per cent, as shown in Table 3.10. However, mining and construction, which have higher average wages than manufacturing, posted a net gain of 1.6 million jobs for the same period.[32] While manufacturing accounted for more than three-fourths of the jobs in goods production in 1987, the share derived from construction represented one-fifth of that work force. The shift occurring within the sector was most apparent during the mid-1980s, as can be seen in Table 3.12.

Employment in goods production increased by 5.5 per cent or 1.3 million workers between 1970 and 1987 (see Table 3.11). Within manufacturing industries, rapid employment growth has occurred in high technology industries. This growth has been offset by large declines in the older manufacturing industries. In fact, many of the industries showing the greatest employment losses were in the manufacturing area. The primary

TABLE 3.8

Employment Levels by Industry: 1978-1986 (Annual data, numbers in thousands)

Employment status	1978	1979	1980	1981	1982	1983	1984	1985	1986
Total employment	86,697	89,823	90,406	91,156	89,566	90,200	94,495	97,519	99,610
Private sector	71,026	73,876	74,166	75,126	73,729	74,300	78,472	81,125	82,900
Goods producing	25,585	26,461	25,658	25,497	23,813	23,334	24,727	24,859	24,681
Mining	851	958	1,027	1,139	1,128	952	966	927	783
Construction	4,229	4,463	4,346	4,188	3,905	3,948	4,383	4,673	4,904
Manufacturing	20,505	21,040	20,285	20,170	18,781	18,434	19,378	19,260	18,994
Service-producing	61,113	63,363	64,748	65,659	65,753	66,866	69,769	72,660	74,930
Transp./ Utilities	4,923	5,136	5,146	5,165	5,082	4,954	5,159	5,238	5,244
Wholesale trade	4,969	5,204	5,275	5,358	5,278	5,268	5,555	5,717	5,735
Retail trade	14,573	14,989	15,035	15,189	15,179	5,613	16,545	17,356	17,845
Finance, insurance and real estate	4,724	4,975	5,160	5,298	5,341	5,468	5,689	5,955	6,297
Services	16,252	17,112	17,890	18,619	19,036	19,694	20,797	22,000	23,099
Government	15,672	15,947	16,241	16,031	15,837	15,869	16,024	16,394	16,711
Federal	2,753	2,773	2,866	2,772	2,739	2,774	2,807	2,875	2,899
State	3,474	3,541	3,610	3,640	3,640	3,640	3,662	3,734	3,888
Local	9,446	9,633	9,765	9,619	9,458	9,434	9,482	9,687	9,923

Source: U.S. Department of Labor, Monthly Labor Review

TABLE 3.9

Summary of Non-Agricultural Employment by Work Sector (in thousands)

Year	Employ-ment Total	Private Total	Goods Total	Service Total	Service Less Govt.	Govern-ment Total
1970	70880	58325	23578	47302	34749	12553
1971	71214	58331	22935	48278	35398	12880
1972	73675	60341	23668	50007	36674	13333
1973	76790	63058	24893	51897	38165	13732
1974	78265	64095	24794	53471	39301	14170
1975	76945	62259	22600	54345	39660	14685
1976	79382	64511	23352	56030	41159	14871
1977	82471	67344	24346	58125	42998	15127
1978	86697	71026	25585	61113	45440	15673
1979	89823	73876	26461	63363	47416	15947
1980	90406	74166	25658	64748	48507	16241
1981	91156	75126	25497	65659	49628	16031
1982	89566	73729	23813	65753	49916	15837
1983	90200	74330	23334	66866	50996	15870
1984	94496	78472	24727	69769	53746	16023
1985	97519	81125	24859	72660	56266	16394
1986	99610	82900	24681	74930	58220	16710
1987	102112	85049	24884	77228	60166	17062

Change (1970-1987):

%	44.0	45.8	5.5	63.3	73.1	35.9
Net	31232	26724	1306	29926	2541.7	4509

Source: Employment and Earnings 35(March 1988): Table 3.

metal industry was decimated, losing close to 500,000 jobs between 1973 and 1985. Sharp decreases in employment also occurred in apparel, textiles, railroad transportation, and fabricated metals.[33] Also noteworthy were the declines that occurred in the auto industry, involving job losses in both production and management.[34]

Private Service Industries. While the rate of employment in manufacturing has decreased, the volume of service sector employment increased. By 1987 the service sector comprised 59 per cent of all employment within the U.S., as shown in Table 3.13. This represents an increase of 23 million jobs since 1970. During the 1980s alone, almost 10 million more jobs were created by the private service industry. Tables 3.13 through 3. 15 provided

TABLE 3.10

Employment in Goods Production, Percentages of National Employment

Year	Total Employment	Private Goods Total	Total	Mining	Construc-tion	Manufac-turing
1970	100	82.3	33.3	0.9	5.1	27.3
1971	100	81.9	32.2	0.9	5.2	26.2
1972	100	81.9	32.1	0.9	5.3	26.0
1973	100	82.1	32.4	0.8	5.3	26.2
1974	100	81.9	31.7	0.9	5.1	25.7
1975	100	80.9	29.4	1.0	4.6	23.8
1976	100	81.3	29.4	1.0	4.5	23.9
1977	100	81.7	29.5	1.0	4.7	23.9
1978	100	81.9	29.5	1.0	4.9	23.7
1979	100	82.2	29.5	1.1	5.0	23.4
1980	100	82.0	28.4	1.1	4.8	22.4
1981	100	82.4	28.0	1.2	4.6	22.1
1982	100	82.3	26.6	1.3	4.4	21.0
1983	100	82.4	25.9	1.1	4.4	20.4
1984	100	83.0	26.2	1.0	4.6	20.5
1985	100	83.2	25.5	1.0	4.8	19.8
1986	100	83.2	25.0	0.8	5.0	19.2
1987	100	83.4	24.4	0.7	4.9	18.7

Source: Computed from data reported in *Employment and Earnings* 35(March 1988): Table 3.

various breakdowns of the service industries during the period between 1970 and 1987.

Within private services, a sharp net increase in employment is apparent in retail trade where 7.2 million new jobs were created between 1970 and 1987, as seen in Table 3.14. Substantial growth is also evident in the finance, insurance, and real estate industries. While growth has occurred in trans-portation and utilities, producing 863,000 new jobs since 1970, their share of service employment has declined over time remaining below 10 per cent since 1983. Within the "other services" category are the important growth industries of health services and business services. Together they repre-sented about half of the jobs in the other services category in 1987.

Much of the expansion within the private service sector is attributable to three areas: health care, business services, and food services establish-ments. Collectively, they generated more than two and one-half million jobs, but the wage rate for these industries is below the average level for all

TABLE 3.11

Employment in Goods Production by Production Category (in thousands)

Year	Employment Total	Private Total	Goods Total	Mining	Construction	Manufacturing
1970	70880	58325	23578	623	3588	19367
1971	71214	58331	22935	609	3704	18623
1972	73675	60341	23668	628	3889	19151
1973	76790	63058	24893	642	4097	20154
1974	78265	64095	24794	697	4020	20077
1975	76945	62259	22600	752	3525	18323
1976	79382	64511	23352	779	3576	18997
1977	82471	67344	24346	813	3851	19682
1978	86697	71026	25585	851	4229	20505
1979	89823	73876	26461	958	4463	21040
1980	90406	74166	25658	1027	4346	20285
1981	91156	75126	25497	1139	4188	20170
1982	89566	73729	23813	1128	3905	18781
1983	90200	74330	23334	952	3948	18434
1984	94496	78472	24727	966	4383	19378
1985	97519	81125	24859	927	4673	19260
1986	99610	82900	24681	783	4904	18994
1987	102112	85049	24884	741	5031	19112
Change (1970-1987):						
Net	31232	26724	1306	118	1443	-255
%	44.0	45.8	5.5	18.9	40.2	-1.3

Source: Employment and Earnings 35(March 1988): 43.

industries. Within the health services fields, job gains in the private sector were observed in a wide variety of occupations including physicians, dentists, nurses, hospital personnel and medical and dental laboratory personnel.[35]

Public Sector Employment. While the private service sector contains the majority of newly created jobs, the public sector has played an important part in the expansion of U.S. employment. (See Tables 3.16 and 3.17) Between 1970 and 1987, government employment grew from 12.6 million to 17.1 million employees (see Table 3.17). More than half of the net increase of 4,509,000 jobs occurred in local government. In comparison to the public sector growth rate of 36 per cent, the private sector grew by 46 per cent during the same period. However, unlike Sweden and West Germany, the

TABLE 3.12

Employment in Goods Production Category Contributions to Goods Employment

Year	1000s Goods Total	Mining	Construction	Manufacturing
1970	123578	2.6	15.2	82.1
1971	22935	2.7	16.1	81.2
1972	23668	2.7	16.4	80.9
1973	24893	2.6	16.5	81.0
1974	24794	2.8	16.2	81.0
1975	22600	3.3	15.6	81.1
1976	23352	3.3	15.3	81.4
1977	24346	3.3	15.8	80.8
1978	25585	3.3	16.5	80.1
1979	26461	3.6	16.9	79.5
1980	25658	4.0	16.9	79.1
1981	25497	4.5	16.4	79.1
1982	23813	4.7	16.4	78.9
1983	23334	4.1	16.9	79.0
1984	24727	3.9	17.7	78.4
1985	24859	3.7	19.9	77.5
1986	24681	3.2	19.7	77.0
1987	24884	3.0	20.2	76.8

Source: *Employment and Earnings* 35(March 1988): 43.

relative proportion of total public sector employment in the U.S. has remained fairly stable. Government jobs comprised 16.7 per cent of total employment in the United States in 1987; in 1970 the proportion was 17.7 as shown in Table 3.16. Reductions in federal employment in the late 1970s were offset by increases in the state and local work force. While total levels of government employment grew incrementally each year from 1970 to 1980, during the early 1980s small annual decreases in the number of public employees at all levels of government occurred in 1981 and 1982. From 1983 to 1985 the pattern of slight positive growth resumed.[36]

In assessing the volume of public sector employment, it is important to recognize that the current trend toward privatization has shifted the delivery of many publicly funded services at all levels of government to private sector enterprises. Information pertaining to government purchases of services provides some insight into changes in the scope of government operations. Expenditures for services are dichotomized between employee

TABLE 3.13

Private Service Employment Percentages of National Employment

Year	Employ- ment Total	Private Total	Service Less Public	Trans- portation Utilities	Whole- sale Trade	Retail Trade	Finance Insurance Real Est.	Other Svcs.
					Distribution of Private Service			
1970	100	82.3	49.0	6.4	5.6	15.6	5.1	16.3
1971	100	81.9	49.7	6.3	5.6	15.9	5.3	16.6
1972	100	81.9	49.8	6.2	5.6	16.1	5.3	16.7
1973	100	82.1	49.7	6.1	5.6	16.1	5.3	16.7
1974	100	81.9	54.0	6.0	5.7	16.0	5.3	17.2
1975	100	80.9	51.5	5.9	5.7	16.4	5.4	18.1
1976	100	81.3	51.8	5.8	5.7	16.6	5.4	18.3
1977	100	81.7	52.1	5.7	5.7	16.7	5.4	18.6
1978	100	81.9	52.4	5.7	5.7	16.8	5.4	18.7
1979	100	82.2	52.8	5.7	5.8	16.7	5.5	19.1
1980	100	82.0	53.7	5.7	5.8	16.6	5.7	19.8
1981	100	82.4	54.4	5.7	5.9	16.7	5.8	20.4
1982	100	82.3	55.7	5.7	5.9	16.9	6.0	21.3
1983	100	82.4	56.5	5.5	5.8	17.3	6.1	21.8
1984	100	83.0	56.9	5.5	5.9	17.5	6.0	22.0
1985	100	83.2	57.6	5.4	5.9	17.8	6.1	22.5
1986	100	83.2	58.2	5.2	5.9	17.9	6.3	23.0
1987	100	83.3	58.9	5.3	5.7	17.9	6.4	23.6

Source: Computed from data in Employment and Earnings 35(March 1988): 43.

compensation costs and other services. Between 1972 and 1986 total government expenditures for services grew slowly with the strongest increases in expenditures occurring between 1984 and 1986, as shown in Table 3.18. Growth between 1980 and 1982 was modest amounting to $1.8 billion (1972 constant), a .83 per cent increase.[37]

Growth in expenditures for non-employee services has outpaced employee compensation costs in the public sector. Figure 3.D displays the biennial percentage increases in expenditures for employee and non em- ployee costs for all levels of government between 1976 and 1986. As the chart indicates, the amount of growth in government expenditures for employee costs decreased from 1976 to 1980, but increased slightly thereafter. For non-payroll service costs, the rate of growth in government spending also declined in the early 1980s but increased rather sharply from 1982 to 1986.[38]

This trend is most apparent in federal defense service spending where

TABLE 3.14

Private Service Employment by Service Category (in thousands)

Year	Employ- ment Total	Private Services Total	Private Services Less Public	Trans- portation Utilities	Whole- sale Trade	Retail Trade	Finance Insurance Real Est.	Other Svcs.
				Distribution of Private Services				
1970	70880	58325	34749	4515	3993	11047	3645	11548
1971	71214	58331	35398	4476	4001	11351	3772	11797
1972	73675	60341	36674	4541	4113	11836	3908	12276
1973	76790	63058	38165	4656	4277	12329	4046	12857
1974	78265	64095	42301	4725	4433	12554	4148	13441
1975	76945	62259	39660	4542	4415	12645	4165	13892
1976	79382	64511	41159	4582	4546	13209	4271	14551
1977	82471	67344	42998	4713	4708	13808	4467	15303
1978	86697	71026	45440	4923	4969	14573	4724	16252
1979	89823	73876	47416	5136	5204	14989	4975	17112
1980	90406	74166	48507	5146	5275	15035	5160	17890
1981	91156	75126	49628	5165	5358	15189	5298	18619
1982	89566	73729	49916	5082	5278	15179	5341	19036
1983	90200	74330	50996	4954	5268	15613	5468	19694
1984	94496	78472	53746	5159	5555	16545	5689	20797
1985	97519	81125	56266	5238	5717	17356	5955	22000
1986	99610	82900	58220	5244	5735	17843	6297	23097
1987	102112	85049	60166	5378	5797	18264	6589	24137
Change (1970-1987):								
Net	31232	26724	25417	863	1804	7217	2944	12589
%	44.0	45.8	73.1	19.1	45.2	65.3	80.8	109.01

Source: Employment and Earnings 35(March 1988): 43.

other services increased by about 20 per cent biennially between 1980 and 1986, while growth in employee compensation ranged from 5.28 per cent between 1980 and 1982 to 2.3 per cent between 1984 and 1986. In the area of non-defense federal services, expenditures for employee costs declined by 4.60 per cent between 1980 and 1982 and amounted to less than .50 per cent in subsequent biennial periods. At the state and local levels of government, growth in service expenditures resumed after 1982. Between 1984 and 1986 employee compensation increased by 3.4 per cent, while other services grew by almost 15 per cent in the same period, as shown in Table 3.18.

TABLE 3.15

Private Service Employment Category Contribution to Service Employment

		Proportion of Total Private Service Employment				
Year	Private Services 1000s	Transp. and Utilities	Whole- sale Trade	Retail Trade	Finance, Insurance Real Estate	Other Svcs.
1970	34749	13.0	11.5	31.8	10.5	33.2
1971	35398	12.6	11.3	32.1	10.7	33.3
1972	36674	12.4	11.2	32.3	10.7	33.5
1973	38165	12.2	11.2	32.3	10.6	33.7
1974	42301	11.2	10.5	29.7	9.8	31.8
1975	39660	11.5	11.1	31.9	10.5	35.0
1976	41159	11.1	11.0	32.1	10.4	35.4
1977	42998	11.0	10.9	32.1	10.4	35.6
1978	45440	10.8	10.9	32.1	10.4	35.8
1979	47416	10.8	11.0	31.6	10.5	36.1
1980	48507	10.6	10.9	31.0	10.6	36.9
1981	49628	10.4	10.8	30.6	10.7	37.5
1982	49916	10.2	10.6	30.4	10.7	38.1
1983	50996	9.7	10.3	30.6	10.7	38.6
1984	53746	9.6	10.3	30.8	10.6	38.7
1985	56269	9.3	10.2	30.9	10.6	39.1
1986	58217	9.0	10.1	30.7	10.8	39.4
1987	60166	8.9	9.6	30.4	11.0	40.1

Source: Employment and Earnings 35(March 1988): 43.

Change is also evident within the public sector with respect to the functions and services government employees perform, as well as the level at which these services are offered.[39] Presently, more than half of the public work force is found in local government, i.e., municipal and county units. In 1987, state governments employed less than one-fourth of the public work force. Seventeen per cent of all government employees in 1986 were found at the federal level.

The great bulk of American public employees work in state and local education as seen in Figure 3.E. National defense involves 6.6 per cent of the public work force. The second largest functional area is health and hospitals which accounts for about one in ten public employees, the majority of whom work at the state and local levels of government. Police and fire protection involve about 6.5 per cent of the public work force. More than one million

TABLE 3.16

Government Employment by Level as Percentage of National Employment

| | | | | Public Sector Employment | | |
| | Employ-
ment
Total | Private
Total | Govern-
ment
Total | % of National Employment | | |
Year				Federal Total	State Total	Local Total
1970	100	82.3	17.7	3.9	3.8	10.1
1971	100	81.9	18.1	3.8	3.9	10.4
1972	100	81.9	18.1	3.6	3.9	10.6
1973	100	82.1	17.9	3.5	3.8	10.6
1974	100	81.9	18.1	3.5	3.9	10.7
1975	100	80.9	19.1	3.6	4.1	11.4
1976	100	81.3	18.7	3.4	4.1	11.2
1977	100	81.7	18.3	3.3	4.1	10.9
1978	100	81.9	18.1	3.2	4.0	10.9
1979	100	82.2	17.8	3.1	3.9	10.7
1980	100	82.0	18.0	3.2	4.0	10.8
1981	100	82.4	17.6	3.0	4.0	10.6
1982	100	82.3	17.7	3.1	4.1	10.6
1983	100	82.4	17.6	3.1	4.1	10.5
1984	100	83.0	17.0	3.0	4.0	10.0
1985	100	83.2	16.8	3.0	3.9	10.0
1986	100	83.2	16.8	2.9	3.9	10.0
1987	100	83.3	16.7	2.9	3.9	10.0

Source: Computed from data in Employment and Earnings 35(March 1988): 43.

government employees work for the federal postal service, the largest civilian employer in the country.[40]

3.7 Summary

This chapter attempts to identify recent trends in the supply and demand for labor. Growth has been a distinct feature of the American work force with more members of the population participating in the labor market. The American work force has clearly become more diversified. The demand side of the market is less easily characterized. There is an apparent decline in the rate of unemployment in the United States, but some indicators suggest that the demand for labor is not as strong as these figures might indicate. The principal trends in the labor market are presented.

FIGURE 3.D Change in Spending for Service—All Governments: 1970-1986

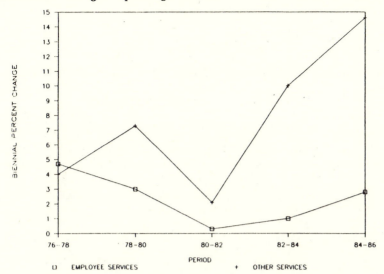

Source: Computed from expenditures in constant dollars given in U.S. Department of Commerce, Bureau of Economic Analysis, *Survey of Current Business, 1983-1987.*

FIGURE 3.E Public Employees by Function, 1985

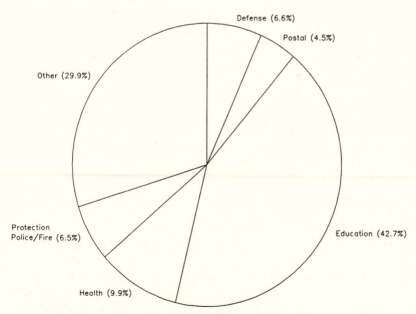

Source: U.S. Department of Commerce, Bureau of Labor Statistics, *Statistical Abstract of the U.S., 1987,* computed from Table 468.

TABLE 3.17

Government Employment by Level (in thousands)

			Public Sector Employment			
Year	Employment Total	Private Total	Government Total	Federal Total	State Total	Local Total
1970	70880	58325	12553	2731	2664	7158
1971	71214	58331	12880	2696	2747	7437
1972	73675	60341	13333	2684	2859	7790
1973	76790	63058	13732	2663	2923	8146
1974	78265	64095	14170	2724	3039	8407
1975	76945	62259	14685	2748	3179	8758
1976	79382	64511	14871	2733	3273	8865
1977	82471	67344	15127	2727	3377	9023
1978	86697	71026	15673	2753	3474	9446
1979	89823	73876	15947	2773	3541	9633
1980	90406	74166	16241	2866	3610	9765
1981	91156	75126	16031	2772	3640	9619
1982	89566	73729	15837	2739	3640	9458
1983	90200	74330	15870	2774	3662	9434
1984	94496	78472	16023	2807	3734	9482
1985	97519	81125	16394	2875	3932	9687
1986	99610	82900	16710	2899	3888	9923
1987	102112	85049	17062	2943	3952	10167

Change (1970-1987)

Net	31232	26724	4509	212	1288	3009
%	44.0	45.8	35.9	7.8	48.3	42.0

Source: Employment and Earnings 35(March 1988): 43.

- A population growth rate of 15.6 per cent translated into 26 million more American workers between 1970 and 1986.
- A shift in the age composition of the work force has occurred. Whereas 21 per cent of the work force was between 25 and 34 years of age in 1970, in 1987 this age group represented 29 per cent of all workers. At the same time older workers have become a smaller proportion of the labor force. Those over 55 years of age represented 18 per cent of the work force in 1960, while in 1987 their share of the work force was only 13 per cent.

TABLE 3.18

Biennial Change in Government Purchases of Services from 1976 to 1986

Period	Federal Employee	Defense Other	Federal Employee	Non-Defense Other	State and Local Employee Other		Total
			Per cent change in expenditures				
1976-78	-.3	-2.8	4.29	14.74	4.19	3.77	3.12
1978-80	0	16.42	2.35	10.09	4.02	2.42	4.12
1980-82	5.28	19.87	-4.60	-15.70	-.38	.30	.83
1982-84	3.24	21.92	.18	8.82	.19	3.83	3.70
1984-86	2.30	20.61	.30	2.60	3.40	14.95	6.17

Source: Computed from U.S. Department of Commerce, Bureau of Economic Analysis, Survey of Current Business, July 1983, July 1985, July 1987. Computations based on tables of expenditures in billions of constant dollars.

• As in other countries, there is a trend toward equalization between the sexes with respect to rates of participation. More than two-thirds of American women were in the work force in 1986. Women's share of the total labor force now equals 44 per cent. Differences related to child rearing responsibilities do not appear significant at present.
• At the same time, male labor force participation rates have declined in the U.S. as they have elsewhere. About three-fourths of all men are currently members of the labor force. This is a reduction of nine per cent since 1950.
• Immigration, particularly on the part of Hispanic persons from Central and South America is a significant factor in the growth of the U.S. labor supply. About 20 per cent of the growth in labor supply between 1983 and 1987 is attributed to Hispanic immigrants.
• Part-time employment has become increasingly important in the U.S. labor market, rising from 14 per cent of the work force in 1970 to 18 per cent in 1987. Part-time workers are predominantly female, but there is trend toward greater rates of part time employment among men.
• Involuntary part-time employment which climbed sharply as a result of the recession of 1981-1982, has declined in recent years, but it has not returned to pre-recession levels.

• Rising levels of temporary employment have changed the profile of the present work force. Estimates of the size of the temporary work force range from 455,000 to 689,000 workers.

• The U.S. has shared the experience of a shift toward service industries in the demand for labor.

• Goods production jobs declined from one-third to one-fourth of U.S. employment between 1970 and 1987. Within this sector manufacturing industries experienced the sharpest declines, dropping from 27 per cent of the national work force to 19 percent. Some increase in the size of the work force involved in mining and construction has reduced the net loss for the goods sector.

• Within the service sector, the growth leaders have been health, business services, and education.

• The public sector share of national employment appears to have remained stable over time, but there has been some redistribution of workers from the federal level to the state and local levels of government.

• In government, growth in non-employee compensation service costs have outpaced payroll costs during the 1980s, reflecting the trend toward privatization of public services in the U.S.

4
Changes in
Labor Market Dynamics

In this chapter, three indicators of labor market dynamics are presented in order to give some insight into the flexibility and rigidity of the American labor market. In the first section, the relationship between unemployment levels and the number of jobs available is discussed as an indicator of the extent to which the supply and demand for labor are matched. The second section provides information pertaining to wage differentials among American workers and the relative position of different groups of workers over time. The third indicator of labor market dynamics presented is the pattern of occupational and geographic mobility. Labor market segmentation, mismatches between the supply and demand for labor, reduces the efficiency of the market, while the propensity of workers to move away from job poor areas or to change to occupations with greater employment opportunities enhances market flexibility.

4.1 Relationship of Unemployment Level to Vacancy Rate

The relationship between the number of job vacancies in the labor market and the rate of unemployment in the work force is one indicator of the market's level of efficiency. Market efficiency may be affected by structural change including changes in the industrial composition of the demand structure and by labor market segmentation. Supply factors relating to the skills and experience of labor are factors. The extent to which the demand for jobs is effectively communicated to those available for work also influences the level of match.

The question of interest is the extent to which members of the work force have the skills that are in demand and the ability of the market system to match qualified workers with open positions. In that the changes in the industrial structure discussed earlier make the skills and experience of certain workers obsolete, some mismatch must exist between the qualifications of segments of the work force and the tasks and duties employers want performed.

The relationship between available jobs in a labor market and unemployment can be represented by the equation

$$E = J - V = L - U$$

where E represents the number of persons employed, J equals the demand for labor, V equals the number of vacant positions, L represents the size of the labor force, and U equals the number of persons unemployed.[41] The extent to which job vacancies remain unfilled while unemployment persists reflects the "state" of the labor market. Different market "states" can be represented by the graphic relationship between Vacancies and Unemployment, where V is plotted on the X axis and E is plotted along the Y axis. Labor market efficiency is enhanced by policies that maximize the match between available workers and job vacancies; thus market efficiency at different time periods can be measured by the intercept point between V and U.[42]

The interpretation of the relationship between given levels of unemployment and vacancies is based on the theories of Lord Beveridge, the British statistician and economist. According to Beveridge, an outward drift of the curve suggests a decrease in market efficiency. Points on the Beveridge Curve where the number of unemployed exceeds the number of available jobs suggest inadequate demand for labor or excessive wage rates. On the other hand, where the number of job vacancies is greater than the number of unemployed, demand for labor is excessive and likely to produce inflationary pressure on wages.

In the case of the United States, official national statistics for job vacancies are not compiled and thus surrogate measures of job openings must be found. Two different indicators of vacancies are used. The first is the number of job openings received by the U.S. Employment Service (USES). The second is the index of help wanted ads which is produced by the Conference Board from major national newspapers. Both indicators involve some measurement error. The openings reported to the USES are thought to represent disproportionately manual and low skilled jobs while newspaper advertisements are thought to overrepresent white collar positions. Competition among newspaper publishers, federal equal employment opportunity guidelines for advertising jobs, and changes in the occupational structure of the market are three factors which may influence the volume of "help wanted" newspaper ads over time. Abraham has demonstrated that these factors are significant but they do not alter general pattern of association.[43]

Information pertaining to the number of job vacancies and the rate of unemployment is reported by year in Table 4.1. Both indicators of vacancy show considerable fluctuation over the 18-year period. The seasonally adjusted Help Wanted Ad Index appears to be responsive to three of the four recessions that occurred within this period, the exception being the

TABLE 4.1

Job Openings and Unemployment Levels by Year: 1970-1987

Year	Job Openings Received by US Employment Service (1000)	Index of News-Paper Help Wanted Ads (1000)[a]	Normalized Ad Index	Level of Unemployment	
				Per Cent	Number
1987	——	153	1.54	6.2	7,425
1986	6968	138	1.38	7.0	8,237
1985	6950	139	1.42	7.1	8,312
1984	5144	131	1.38	7.5	8,539
1983	6494	95	1.06	9.6	10,717
1982	6150	86	.96	9.7	10,678
1981	7548	118	1.29	7.6	8,237
1980	8122	128	1.42	7.1	7,637
1979	9477	157	1.75	5.8	6,317
1978	9534	149	1.72	6.1	6,047
1977	8396	118	1.43	7.1	6,855
1976	7668	95	1.20	7.7	7,288
1975	7889	80	1.04	8.5	7,830
1974	9439	110	1.41	5.6	5,076
1973	9443	126	1.64	4.9	4,304
1972	7550	103	1.40	5.6	4,840
1971	5999	83	1.16	5.9	4,994
1970	6130	93	1.31	4.9	4,088

[a]Ad index obtained from the Conference Board, seasonally adjusted.
Sources: U.S. Department of Commerce, Bureau of the Census, Statistical Abstract of the U.S., 1985, Tables 686 and 687; U.S. Department of Labor, Bureau of Labor Statistics, News, 87-67, February 1987, and 85-25, January 1985; Monthly Labor Review, 111(October 1988): 68.

seven-month recession lasting between January and July of 1980. However, a low volume of ads was observed in 1971, 1975, and 1982. The relationship between the normalized index of Help Wanted Ads and rate of unemployment is illustrated in Figure 4.A. The normalized index is obtained by dividing the ad index by non-agricultural employment in millions.

As Figure 4.A reveals, an outward and upward shift in the Beveridge curve is apparent over time in the United States indicating a decrease in overall market efficiency. The positions to the right of the 45 degree angle indicate that a demand deficiency existed in the mid-1970s and early 1980s. The positions to the left of the 45 degree angle show that vacancies exceeded employment demand in the late 1970s indicating overheated demand and inadequate linkage between employers and potential employees. Abraham shows that this trend has been underway since the 1950s. The direction of the shift indicates growing incongruity between the demand for labor and the available human resources, although in the most recent two years, 1986 and 1987, an inward movement is apparent reflecting the decline in unemployment levels which is currently underway in the United States. The upward movement in 1987 suggests a sharp increase in the number of job

FIGURE 4.A Unemployment and Vacancies in the US: 1970 - 1987

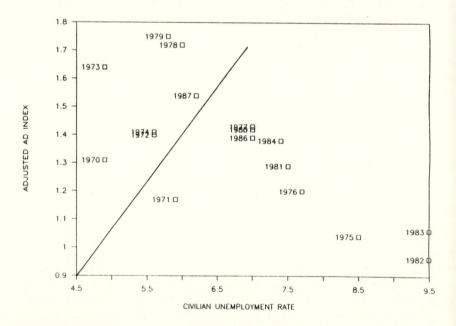

Source: See Table 4.1

vacancies. Similarly, the Bureau of Labor Statistic's Index of Diffusion, which reflects expansion in non-agricultural employment, indicates a sharp increase in industrial employment began in mid-1987. Abraham's state-level analysis concludes that greater regional economic dispersion is an important factor in accounting for the outward shift in the Beveridge Curve.[44]

This interpretation is consistent with Harrison and Bluestone's analysis which indicates that shifts in the interregional distribution of low-paying jobs have occurred. In the early 1960s, southern workers were most likely to occupy low wage positions. In the current decade, the midwest, which relies so heavily on manufacturing, is the most over-represented section in the distribution of low wage jobs. While the pattern for western states exhibits little change, among the northeastern states, which have consistently had the smallest share of low-paying jobs, an upward trend in the share of low wage jobs was evident between 1963 and 1979, but recovery is apparent in the most recent data which indicate that an improvement in pay rates has occurred.[45]

In judging regional comparisons in the U.S., it is important to recognize that the cost of living varies considerably across the nation and to some extent moderates the apparent advantage of workers in the northeast and the disadvantage of individuals working in the south. On the other hand, Harrison and Bluestone's analysis shows the differences among the regions in the distribution of national wealth.

4.2 Wage Differentials

The size of wage differentials among different categories of workers has declined over time, and the ratio of non-skilled to skilled manual workers' wages rose by a relatively high amount over the last two decades. Disparities between classes of workers are greater in the private sector than in government.[46]

Wage Rates in Private Industry. When hourly earnings are viewed in constant dollars, it appears that American workers have lost some earning power over the last ten years. The data reported here indicate a decline in actual earnings occurred after 1975 and a smaller reduction was experienced between 1985 and 1987 (See Table 4.2 and Figure 4.B). While the average hourly wage in 1970 was $5.04, in 1987 the average worker received $4.86 per hour, a reduction of about 4 per cent. Two industries are exceptions to this general downward trend: mining and transportation/public utilities. Of the two, mining has shown the strongest gains in wages with an increase of 12 per cent between 1970 and 1987. Transportation and

56

public utilities workers experienced a gain of about 8 per cent in their hourly earnings. Although the manufacturing industry has lost a large number of jobs, wages have been rather stable in that industry.

TABLE 4.2

Average Hourly Earnings in Constant (1977) Dollars, by Private Industry Group, 1970-1987 Selected Years

	1970	1975	1980	1985	1987
Average Hourly Earnings	5.04	5.10	4.89	4.88	4.86
Manufacturing	5.23	5.44	5.34	5.43	5.37
Mining	6.01	6.70	6.74	6.83	6.74
Construction	8.17	8.23	7.30	7.01	6.86
Transportation, Utilities	6.01	6.62	6.52	6.50	6.51
Wholesale trade	5.37	5.33	5.11	5.22	5.21
Retail trade	3.81	3.78	3.59	3.38	3.32
Finance, Insurance, Real estate	4.79	4.57	4.25	4.52	4.75
Services	4.38	4.53	4.30	4.50	4.59

Sources: U.S. Department of Commerce, Bureau of the Census, *Statistical Abstract of the U.S.*, 1987, Table 676; *Employment and Earnings* 35(March 1988): 80. Data are for production and non-supervisory workers.

Among non-supervisory private industry workers, those in the mining, transportation, and construction industries have had the highest hourly wages. The lowest wages are found in services and the retail trades. These patterns are consistent over time as the data in Table 4.3 indicate. Between 1970 and 1987 there has been very little change in the relative size of wage differentials between the highest and lowest paid industries as shown in Table 4.3. The ratio of earnings is about .48. Thus on this indicator of disparity among workers, very little change is evident over the last two decades.

While wage related factors appear to be significant contributors to increased unemployment in some countries, they have not had as great an impact on the joblessness rate in the U.S. Actual wages declined as the rate of unemployment increased, perhaps offsetting greater levels of joblessness. Some conclude that U.S. compensation patterns have become more responsive to market factors.[47]

FIGURE 4.B Private Industry Hourly Wage, Selected Years 1970-1987

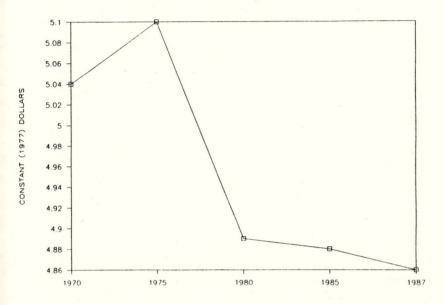

Source: U.S. Department of Commerce, Bureau of the Census, *Statistical Abstract of the U.S.*, 1987, Table 676.

TABLE 4.3

Wage Differentials Between Highest and Lowest Paid Industries

	1970	1975	1980	1985	1987
Differentials (Lowest/Highest)	47	46	49	48	48

Sources: U.S. Department of Commerce, Bureau of the Census, *Statistical Abstract of the U.S.*, 1987, Table 676; *Employment and Earnings* 35(March 1988): 80. Data are for production and non-supervisory workers.

Wage Rates and Unemployment Levels. Although the rate of unemployment declined through the late 1980s, expected increases in wage levels have not been apparent. A number of explanations have been offered for this curious inconsistency with labor market theory (shortages in the supply of labor should drive up the rate of pay as employers compete for human resources), but none is satisfactory. Historically, unemployment levels of 6 per cent have produced an increase in the rate of wage inflation. There is no evidence to date of upward movement in wages although unemployment fell below 6 per cent at the end of 1987.

One explanation for non-increasing wage rates is that the supply of labor is not as limited as rates of unemployment seem to suggest. Evidence of underemployment in the form of involuntary part-time employment, the number of discouraged workers, the increase in temporary and part-time jobs, and growth in the number of low wage jobs in metropolitan areas support this argument.[48]

Increases in the proportion of payroll attributable to non-wage costs are also indicators of growth in compensation rates. Employers are the principal sponsor of individual health insurance in the U.S., and increases in the amount of paid leave as well as increasing private pension costs are important factors in assessing total compensation. Statistics pertaining to employer costs for production workers corrected for the rate of inflation indicate that non-wage costs do not offset declines in wage rates. The changes in the adjusted Employer Cost Index (ECI) from 1971 to 1987 are not significantly correlated with the rate of unemployment. Table 4.4 and Figure 4.C show the annual per cent change in the adjusted ECI along with the unemployment rate for the civilian population.

Female-Male Earnings Differential. When median earnings between the sexes for full-time employees are compared over time similar patterns are observed using either annual or weekly earnings. The ratio of women's annual earnings to men's annual earnings in the mid-1960s was 58 per cent, marking a decline of several percentage points from the previous decade. Women continued to earn a rather low proportion of men's earnings through the mid-1970s, but from the late 1970s forward a reduction in the size of the wage gap between male and female earnings is apparent. Estimates for 1986 indicate that women earned about 69 per cent as much as men annually.

Among industrial workers in 1986, women's pay averaged 70 per cent of men's pay. This reflects an improvement of 14 per cent in the wage gap. In government, women earned 80 per cent as much as men, on the average in 1986. This reflects substantial improvement in the size of both state and local and federal wage differentials. The information is reported below in Table 4.5.

TABLE 4.4

Changes in the Adjusted Employer Cost Index and Unemployment Rates

	Adjusted ECI % Change	Civilian Unemployment %
1987	.20	6.20
1986	1.40	7.00
1985	-.40	7.10
1984	1.90	7.40
1983	2.60	9.50
1982	.60	9.50
1981	.40	7.50
1980	-3.70	7.00
1979	-2.50	5.80
1978	.10	6.00
1977	.55	7.00
1976	1.40	7.70
1975	-14.90	8.50
1974	-.20	5.60
1973	-.80	4.90
1972	2.60	5.60
1971	12.10	5.90

Source: U.S. Department of Labor, Bureau of Labor Statistics. The adjusted ECI (Employer Cost Index) is computed from the per cent annual change in the total compensation cost for private industry workers minus the per cent change in the Consumer Price Index (author's computations).

Earnings Differentials by Race. Disparities in earnings related to race are generally smaller than those between the sexes but they have not shown as much improvement over time. Table 4. 6 reports related data. Among industrial workers, blacks earned 78 per cent as much as whites in 1986. This is an improvement of 4 per cent from 1977. In the federal government, black earnings were 86 per cent of white's earnings, reflecting a loss in relative position of five per cent from 1977. At the state and local levels of government there were no improvements over time and blacks earned 81 per cent as much as whites.

When women are considered separately, a sharp increase in the ratio of earnings by female minority group members relative to white females is apparent from 1955 forward. The ratio of white to non-white female

60

FIGURE 4.C Change in Adjusted ECI and Unemployment, 1971-1987

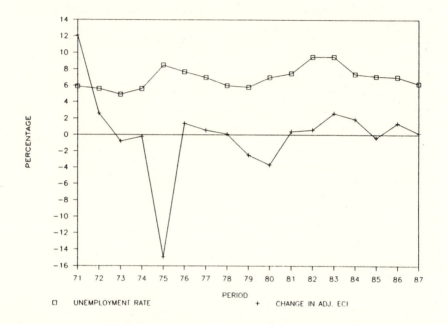

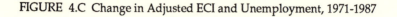

earnings equaled about .70 in 1960, but drifted between 92 and 99 per cent since the mid-1970s. The U.S. Council of Economic Advisers partly attributes these improvements in the size of earnings differentials among women of different racial groups to increased levels of educational attainment among minority females.[49]

At the same time, the proportion of low-paying jobs associated with white and non-white women has also equalized over time. The sharp differences between the races which were apparent in the early 1960s declined rapidly over that decade and by 1979 were no longer evident. Collectively, women were more likely than men to hold low paying jobs. In 1985, women were more than twice as likely as white men to hold jobs paying less than $7,400 per year.[50] According to the Bureau of Labor Statistics, 19 per cent of white working women and 27 per cent of black women earned less than $200 per week in 1986. Among white males, only 8 per cent were at this wage level. Conversely, 41 per cent of white males earned $500 or more per week, while only 15 per cent of white females and 11 per cent of black females had equivalent earnings.[51]

TABLE 4.5

American Women's Earnings as a Percentage of Men's Earnings by Sector of Employment for Full-Time Employees: 1977 and 1986

Sector	1977 %	1986 %
Industry	56	70
Federal Government	71	80
State & Local Gov't.	73	80

Source: U.S. Department of Commerce, Bureau of the Census, *Consumer Income*, Current Population Reports, Series P-60, No. 118, and computed from unpublished data from the Current Population Survey.

TABLE 4.6

Earnings Differentials by Race, Blacks' Median Earnings as a Percentage of Whites by Sector for Full-Time Employees: 1977 and 1986

Sector	1977 %	1986 %
Industry	74	78
Federal Government	91	86
State & Local Gov't.	81	81

Source: U.S. Department of Commerce, Bureau of the Census, *Consumer Income*, Current Population Reports, Series P-60, No. 118, and computed from unpublished data from the Current Population Survey.

4.3 Mobility Factors Affecting the Labor Pool

Americans think of themselves as highly mobile both in terms of geographic relocation and occupational change. Statistical evidence generally supports these perceptions, but persons in some other countries are as mobile or more mobile than Americans. Job tenure levels between Americans and Australians are similar, although Australians have demonstrated lower levels of seniority with a particular employer than Americans.

Although the average current job tenure in the U.S. is 7.2 years, Australians had an average tenure rate of 6.6 years in 1985. The differences were evident for both sexes. In comparison with Japanese, Belgian, Irish, and German workers, Americans have lower average tenure rates.[52]

Occupational Mobility. Transitions workers make from one occupation to another are among the most important aspects of labor market flexibility in that they increase the likelihood of achieving a match between the kinds of workers seeking jobs and the sort of jobs available. A high propensity for occupational change is an advantage during periods of rapid technological change in particular. Between January of 1986 and January of 1987, about 10 per cent of all American workers changed their occupations (see Table 4.7). A similar rate occurred in 1983. Most workers make the transition from one occupation to another in order to improve their pay level or working conditions, but a small portion are forced to change their line of work as a result of structural change or lay-off. For half of all persons who changed occupations between 1986 and 1987, the net result was an increase in earnings. About 22 per cent experienced no change in earnings, while 29 per cent suffered a wage loss. Displaced workers are more likely to experience an earnings shortfall than others.

Certain individual characteristics are related to changes in occupational status; among these are age, sex, and profession. Of the three, age is the most important characteristic in explaining individual mobility. Younger workers who have fewer family obligations and lower career investments with a particular employer are much more mobile than older persons. Occupational mobility rates are highest among workers under 25 years of age and decline after 34 years of age. This pattern has been consistent over the last three decades.[53]

A person's sex is related to his or her rate of occupational mobility, although the direction of the relationship has changed over time, as Table

TABLE 4.7

Adult Occupational Mobility Rates by Sex, for Selected Time Periods

	1965-66	1972-73	1977-78	1980-81	1982-83	1986-87
Males	9.9	9.2	11.6	10.1	9.3	9.6
Females	6.9	8.4	11.7	11.4	9.9	10.4

Sources: Monthly Labor Review 107(October 1984): 22; U.S. Department of Labor, Bureau of Labor Statistics, *News*, 87-452, October 1987.

4.7 indicates. Although men historically experienced more occupational change than women, this pattern reversed in the mid-1970s and since then women's rate of occupational mobility has been slightly higher than men's rate. Between 1986 and 1987, 10.4 per cent of employed women experienced a change in occupation while the rate was only 9.6 per cent for men. In comparison, between 1965 and 1966, 9.9 per cent of all employed men changed occupations while only 6.9 per cent of working women did. The gain for women is an increase of 3.5 per cent. More men (30%) than women (21 %) have attained ten years of employment with the same employer but the differences between the sexes in job tenure are less apparent among younger workers.

Several factors may account for increased occupational mobility among women. Women's work histories[54] and their greater likelihood to enter the growing service sector are factors accounting for greater movement. Greater access to professional and managerial jobs are components of upward mobility and they may be attributed to reductions in the rate of discrimination, higher educational achievements, and the impact of anti-discrimination and affirmative action legislation regulating employment.[55]

A person's profession is a factor in explaining the rate of occupational mobility. The lowest rates of change are among those workers in the primary sector (agriculture, forestry and fishing), the highest rates occur among persons in service professions. Among white collar workers, persons in managerial work, are less likely to switch to other types of work than clericals and to some extent, professional workers. Persons in the trades and crafts are less likely to experience an occupational change than others and have higher rates of tenure on their current job than clerical or service workers.[56]

When mobility rates are examined by race, blacks have the lowest levels of occupational mobility among workers in almost every category.[57] However, periods of tenure with a single employer do not differ sharply among black and white workers.[58]

Geographic Mobility. Americans have relatively high rates of geographic mobility. They are more likely to relocate in a given year and experience more changes of residence within their lifetimes than people in many other countries. Americans appear to have a greater propensity to migrate long distances than other people, including Swedes. A number of factors contribute to relatively higher rates of spatial mobility in the United States. One factor is that there is a large portion of Americans who frequently relocate. A second factor is the economic development of the southern and western states, and the periods of decline suffered by northern and midwestern industrial states. Third, Americans appear to have a greater propensity to move at different life cycle stages than persons in some other countries.[59]   Finally, the availability of housing stock is not as restrictive in the U.S. as it is in other countries. These characteristics are an advantage to a national economy during periods of structural change.

There have been some distinct trends in the pattern of spatial mobility over the last three decades. During the 1950s and 1960s strong rates of movement into metropolitan areas were apparent. Between 1960 and 1970, the annual growth rate for non-urban areas was only 2.5 per cent, compared to a rate of 16.1 per year in metropolitan areas. A component of this migration was the substantial exodus of blacks and other workers from agricultural areas to industrial centers. During the 1960s and continuing into the next decade, many manufacturing activities moved out of central cities.[60]

An unanticipated reversal in the flow of migration and a reduction in the overall rate of mobility occurred during the 1970s when the rate of growth in non-urban areas exceeded the metropolitan growth rate. This exodus from urban areas, which was predominantly motivated by non-economic reasons, declined toward the end of the decade. Structural changes in the economy became important determinants in the flow of labor from the declining manufacturing centers of the northeast and midwest to the economically developing states in the south and west. The non-urban growth rate between 1970 and 1980 was 13.5 per cent each year; while metropolitan growth occurred at an average annual rate of 10.1 per cent yearly. During the 1980s the rate of growth has been a few percentage points larger for metropolitan areas than non-urban areas.[61]

In this decade, about 17 per cent of the population has changed its place of residence each year. The rate is slightly lower than the level of spatial mobility observed in previous periods. The data in Table 4.8 report both the rate and volume of geographic mobility in the U.S. from 1950 to 1985.

From 1984 to 1985, 46 million Americans changed their place of residence. This number represents about 20 per cent of the population, which is a slight increase over previous years. Higher mortgage rates are thought to account for slightly lower mobility rates in the early 1980s. About 15 million of those who moved left their previous home county.

Individual characteristics are associated with mobility. Age is strongly related to the propensity to move in the U.S. as it is in other countries. Younger persons, particularly those in their twenties, have historically shown a greater receptivity to geographic change than persons 35 years of age and older. This is the period when individuals terminate their schooling, fulfill their military obligations, start careers, and first marry, all of which are factors associated with starting a new household or changing location. It can generally be said that persons without high school degrees are less mobile than persons with more years of schooling. For those

TABLE 4.8

Annual Geographic Mobility Rates for Selected One-Year Periods

Mobility Period	Total Volume of Movers 1000s	Percentage of Population
1984-85	46,000	20
1983-84	39,379	17
1982-83	37,408	17
1981-82	38,127	17
1980-81	38,200	17
1975-76	36,793	18
1970-71	37,705	19
1965-66	37,586	20
1960-61	36,533	21
1955-56	34,040	21
1950-51	31,464	21

Source: U.S. Department of Commerce, Geographical Mobility, Current Population Reports, Series P-20, No. 407, September 1986.

between 20 and 24 years of age the mobility rate was 38 per cent; while 36 per cent of those between 25 and 29 undertook a change of residence. The rates for older persons were lower with 30 per cent of those in the 20- to 40-year-old age group moving and 9 per cent of those between 45 and 64 changing residence. Between 1984 and 1985, men were slightly more mobile than women.[62] Interstate migration is generally higher for Caucasians than it is for blacks and members of other minorities.

With respect to income, members of the middle class are more likely to relocate than persons with higher or lower income levels.[63] In recent years about one-fifth of the civilian work force moves annually. Of those relocating, persons who are jobless are more mobile than those who are employed.[64] But about half of all those who relocate cite employment related factors as their principal reason for moving.[65]

Internal Labor Markets. Given the amount of mobility apparent in the American work force, the importance of single organizations in terms of individual careers is of particular interest. Internal labor markets are defined by organizations and governed by administrative policies. They are distinct from external labor markets in the way they operate in that where organizational policies structure a closed personnel system, encouraging or requiring promotion from within to fill non-entry positions, a portion of the work force is sheltered from the competition of market forces. Organizational policies and employment laws pertaining to job security, transfer, reductions in force, as well as upward mobility structures affect the strength of internal markets.

Changes in the structure of the labor market and the composition of the work force should translate into changes in the extent to which individuals rely upon internal labor markets for career advancement.[66] On the one hand, industrial structures affect the direction of career paths and on the other hand, organizational size and industrial complexity contribute to the range of opportunity within a particular organization. As the balance of peripheral and core workers in the labor force changes, the proportion of workers who have long tenure with a single employer may decline. The impact of low organizational commitment on market efficiency is a subject of discussion.

In examining the data pertaining to job tenure reported in Table 4.9, it should be noted that a change in the survey instrument occurred in 1983, making information more precisely related to a single employer. In previous years, the question referred to tenure in a person's current job. This change probably lowers the median years with a particular employer since the construct is more precisely defined after 1983.

Overall, the level of job tenure exhibited by U.S. workers appears to be slightly higher in 1987 than it was in 1973. For the total work force, the increase amounts to .3 years. Among men, an increase of .4 years occurred and for women an increase of .8 is indicated. Median years with an employer appear to be recovering from declines that occurred in the late 1970s and early 1980s. Loyalty to a single employer competes with other factors in determining the job tenure of particular workers. Among these are broad structural changes which displace employees who formerly had

TABLE 4.9

Job Tenure Rates Among American Workers, 1973-1987 Median Years in January

	Total	Males	Females
1987	4.2	5.0	3.6
1983	4.4	5.1	3.7
1981	3.2	4.0	2.5
1978	3.8	4.5	2.6
1973	3.9	4.6	2.8

Source: U.S. Department of Labor, Bureau of Labor Statistics.

consistent employment with the same business; entrance into the labor force of workers seeking only part-time or temporary work arrangements; economic conditions that limit the possibility of securing full-time work and affect the rate of unemployment in the external market, and changes in the age structure of the work force, where younger workers who normally have less seniority with an employer become more dominant in work force composition.

When the data are examined by age, a different picture emerges, as seen in Table 4.10. The median job tenure for white workers between 35 and 44 years and between 45 and 54 years of age shows an apparent increase in the duration of employment with a single employer among members of both sexes in the most recent data. Women have lower rates of job tenure than men have in both age groups. (The increments after 1981 are deflated by the change in question wording in that period.) These statistics suggest that demographic factors including the changing age composition of the work force, the larger number of workers below 35 years of age, and the larger female share of the work force partly explain the overall population trend in job seniority.

TABLE 4.10

Median Years of Job Tenure Among White Workers by Sex and Age

Year	35-44 Years		45-54 Years	
	Male	Female	Male	Female
1987	7.7	4.7	12.7	7.0
1981	6.7	3.3	11.2	5.7
1973	6.8	3.4	11.7	5.8

Source: U.S. Department of Labor, Bureau of Labor Statistics.

4.4 Summary

In this chapter three indicators of labor market flexibility have been considered. These were the relationship between job vacancies and the rate of unemployment, the structure of wages, and the rate of mobility among the work force. The key findings are:

• There has been an apparent decrease during the first half of the 1980s in the the efficiency of the American labor market reflected in an upward and outward shift of the Beveridge Curve. This trend needs to be monitored, given the reductions in 1987 and 1988 in unemployment.

• The wage structure in the United States evidences a slight decline in hourly earnings among workers.

• Differentials in earnings vary for different groups of workers. Between the highest and lowest paid industries there has been little change in earnings differentials. For demographic groups, disparities persist between men and women but are not as great between the races. One group whose wage position has improved over time is the black female.

• Unlike other work forces, the American case shows little long term decline in occupational mobility and the propensity to move is as great among females as it is among males.

• Overall, job tenure has declined for the American work force, but prime age white workers show longer commitment to a single employer over time and this suggests that internal labor markets have increased in importance for some segments of the American work force. Shifts in the age composition of the labor pool are likely to alter this pattern of job tenure.

• During the first half of the 1980s, geographic mobility among Americans was suppressed, but most recent data indicate a return to previous levels of migration.

5
The Structure and
Dynamics of Unemployment

The rate of unemployment in the United States has historically been high in comparison with some other OECD countries, but the duration of unemployment experienced by single individuals has generally been lower. During the mid-1980s the rate of unemployment improved overall in the United States. In 1986, the national unemployment rate equaled 7 per cent of the civilian work force which compares rather favorably to the trends observed in OECD nations.[67] During 1987, the rate of unemployment continued to decline, remaining below 6 per cent of the work force during the last quarter of 1987 and through 1988. In 1987, the level of unemployment fell below eight million cases for the first time this decade affecting 7.4 million Americans in 1987 (see Table 5.1).

The current pattern of decline in the rate of unemployment is somewhat puzzling in that it runs counter to Okun's Law, which posits that the rate of growth in the GNP determines the rate of change in unemployment. Okun's original formula specified a 4 per cent rate of growth to reduce the level of unemployment, but later revisions to this estimate allowed that a 2.5 rate of growth in GNP was sufficient to reduce the rate of unemployment. Now, even that revised formula appears to have broken down in that unemployment has declined more rapidly than would be anticipated during a period of weak economic growth.[68]

At the same time, the declines occurring in the rate of unemployment have not been associated with an increase in the rate of wage inflation. In the current period, there is an apparent decline in the nonaccelerating inflation rate of unemployment (NAIRU), which is discussed in Chapter 4.

Reasons for Unemployment. In recent years, about half of those who are jobless cite involuntary reasons, as the data reported in Table 5.1 indicate. In 1982 and 1983, the number of involuntary separations as a proportion of all unemployment was estimated at almost 60 per cent. The proportion of unemployed workers who lost their jobs due to layoffs was highest in the periods after the 17-month 1973-1975 recession and after the equally long 1981-1982 recession at 21 per cent and 20 per cent respectively. The proportion of lay-offs was also high in 1980, at 19 per cent of all unemployed workers and this marks the end of a shorter recessionary period.

TABLE 5.1

Reasons for Unemployment as a Percentage of Civilian Unemployed, 1970-1987

	1970	1975	1980	1981	1982	1983	1984	1985	1986	1987
Job Losers	44	55	52	52	59	58	52	50	49	47
Lay-offs	16	21	19	17	20	17	14	14	13	13
Job Leavers	13	10	12	11	8	8	10	11	12	13
Re-Entrants	30	24	25	25	22	22	26	27	26	27
New Eentrants	12	10	11	12	11	11	13	12	12	12
Civilian Unemployed 1000s	4093	5016	7637	8273	10678	10717	8539	8312	8237	7425

Note: Totals may not add to 100% due to rounding.
Sources: U.S. Department of Labor, Bureau of Labor Statistics, *Labor Force Statistics Derived from the Current Population Survey*, Table B-25, and *Employment Situation*, November 1987; *Monthly Labor Review* 110(September 1987): 94 and 111(February 1988): 90; U.S. Department of Commerce, Bureau of the Census, *Statistical Abstract of the U.S.*, 1985, Table 681.

About one in ten unemployed persons quit their former job. New entrants and re-entrants into the work force accounted for about 40 per cent of the unemployed, as shown in Table 5.1. These proportions have been rather stable in the years shown between 1970 and 1987. In the following section information about the demographic distribution of the unemployment experience is presented followed by a discussion of the broad dynamics of unemployment.

5.1 The Distribution of Unemployment

Unemployment is a condition that falls unevenly upon certain segments of the American work force. Recognition of the discriminating aspects of joblessness led to the promulgation of a number of government programs during the 1960s and 1970s which sought to reduce the level of unemployment among particular groups or in economically distressed areas. Among those groups with traditionally high rates of unemployment are youth, blacks, and older workers. Women have historically had higher rates of unemployment than men, but the male rate of unemployment exceeded women's in 1982. Among the new jobless are males of prime working-age who, as a consequence of structural changes in U.S. industries, find little demand for their skills and experience. In the following section, a closer examination of the pattern demographic unemployment is made.

Unemployment among Age Cohorts. Age is associated with different rates of unemployment as the data reported in Table 5.2 indicate. The lowest levels of employment for either sex are found among persons in the 55 and over age category, the highest levels of unemployment occur among teenagers. Relative to prime age males, those between 35 and 44 years of age, young males are much more likely to experience unemployment as the group ratios indicate. Older male workers are not as likely to experience unemployment relative to prime age males in the U.S. as they are in other countries although attrition from the work force on the part of discouraged or displaced workers may conceal some joblessness. The group ratios for both males and females are equal to or below 1.0 for persons over 45 years of age. On the other hand, the position of young workers in the U.S., both male and female, relative to prime age males is very disadvantageous.

Youth Unemployment. The rate of unemployment among young people (16-24 years of age) is twice as great as the rate for those more than 24 years old. Almost one in every five young persons seeking a job is unable to find one. In 1980, youths represented about 38 per cent of total unemployment in United States, which is substantially larger than the proportion found in West Germany or Sweden. But within the young population, the ax of unemployment has fallen disproportionately upon black youths since the mid 1950s severing one in two minority youths from the opportunities and benefits of work force participation. The rate of unemployment among nonwhite youths is more than twice as high as the rate among white teenagers.

The labor force behavior of young persons between 20 and 24 years of age can be distinguished from teenagers in that they have lower levels of unemployment. In 1985, 18.6 per cent of the persons in this age category were jobless. As was the case with teenagers, whites fared substantially

TABLE 5.2

Average Civilian Unemployment Rate by Age and Sex for 1987

Males 16 and over	%	Group Ratios[a] to Males 35 - 44 Years	Females 16 and over	%	Group Ratios[a] to Males 35-44 years
	6.2	1.4		6.2	1.4
16-19	17.8	4.0	16-19	15.9	3.6
20-24	9.9	2.2	20-24	9.4	2.1
25-34	5.9	1.3	25-34	6.2	1.4
35-44	4.4	1.0	35-44	4.6	1.0
45-54	4.2	1.0	45-54	3.7	.8
55-64	3.7	.8	55-64	3.1	.7
55-59	3.8	.9	55-59	3.2	.7
60-64	3.6	.8	59-64	3.0	.7
65/+	2.6	.6	65/+	2.4	.5

[a]Unemployment rate for each group divided by the male age 35-44 unemployment rate.
Source: *Employment and Earnings* 35(January 1988): Table 3.

better than minority young people as the data in Table 5.3 indicate. About 20 per cent of long term unemployment was composed of young people in 1986.[69] As the data reported in Table 5.3 reveal, the rate of unemployment among non-white teenagers grew steadily in the past, almost doubling between 1965 and 1985. But thereafter minority youths benefited from the general decline in U.S. unemployment, experiencing unemployment rates below those observed in 1975. In 1987 the gap between white and non-white youth was the lowest for the 1980s but the unemployment ratio between the races has exceeded 2.0. for both age groups in this decade.

Since the late 1960s black teenage girls have slightly exceeded the employment rate of their male counterparts. In 1986, 14.8 per cent of black females were unemployed, compared to a rate of 15.2 per cent for males. Moreover, the duration of unemployment for young black males was 3.5 weeks longer than it was for females.[70] At the same time, unemployment is substantially higher for black females (27 per cent) than it is for white

TABLE 5.3

Youth Unemployment by Race, 1965-1987

Race and Age	1965	1970	1975	1980	1985	1986	1987
White							
16-19	13.4	13.5	17.9	15.5	15.7	15.6	14.4
20-24	——	7.3	12.3	7.6	9.2	8.7	8.0
Black/other							
16-19	26.2	29.1	39.5	38.5	40.2	36.0	32.0
20-24	——	13.8	24.5	23.6	24.5	22.2	19.0
Racial Ratios[a]							
16-19	1.96	2.15	2.21	2.48	2.56	2.31	2.22
20-24	——	1.89	1.99	3.10	2.66	2.55	2.35

[a]Ratio = Black/White for each age cohort.
Sources: U.S. Department of Commerce, Bureau of the Census, *Labor Force Statistics Derived from the Current Population Survey: A Data Book*, vol. 1, and unpublished data; U.S. Department of Commerce, Bureau of the Census, *Statistical Abstract of the U.S.*, 1987, Table 662.

females (9 per cent) between 16 and 24 years old. Low educational attainment indicated by the absence of a high school degree is an explanatory factor, but black unemployment rates are more than twice as large for all levels of education.[71] Among Hispanic young people, males had an unemployment rate of 10.1 per cent in 1986 which was slightly lower than the rate for females.

A number of reasons have been put forward to account for the high rate of unemployment among American youth. These include the size of the youth cohort and the availability of and preference for mature adult workers willing to perform the jobs young people typically fill. Also factors are the wage structure, minimum wage level, and quality of training programs. These factors operate to varying degrees in other countries.[72] In attempting to explain the sharp disparity between young whites and blacks in the United States, education is often cited, as well as experience, geographic location or labor market segmentation, and employer discrimination.[73]

Unemployment among Minority Group Members. Race is a factor in unemployment in the United States, with minority group members generally having larger unemployment levels than whites (Asian-American excepted). Jobless rates have declined since 1983, as shown in Table 5.4. Unemployment among blacks in 1988 was estimated at 11.7 per cent. This was an improvement from 1983 of 7.8 per cent. Unemployment levels for all groups of black workers (males, females and youths) have declined in recent years, but they remain more than twice as high as the white unemployment level. The unemployment rate for blacks has exceeded 10 per cent of the black work force in every year since 1975.

Among Hispanic workers, the rate of unemployment has not been as severe as it has been for blacks. During the 1980s, the unemployment

TABLE 5.4

Unemployment Rates by Race and Hispanic Origin as a Proportion of Population, 1970-1987

Year	Total Unemployed	White	Black/ other	Hispanic	Group Ratios BLK/W	HISP/W
1988	5.5	4.7	11.7	8.2	2.49	1.74
1987	6.2	5.3	13.0	8.8	2.45	1.66
1986	7.0	6.0	14.5	10.6	2.42	1.77
1985	7.1	6.2	15.1	10.5	2.44	1.69
1984	7.4	6.5	15.9	10.7	2.45	1.65
1983	9.5	8.4	19.5	13.7	2.32	1.63
1982	9.5	8.6	18.9	13.8	2.20	1.60
1981	7.5	6.6	14.4	10.4	2.18	1.58
1980	7.0	6.3	14.3	10.1	2.27	1.60
1979	5.8	5.1	12.3	8.3	2.41	1.63
1978	6.0	5.2	12.8	9.1	2.46	1.75
1977	7.0	6.2	13.1	10.1	2.11	1.63
1976	7.7	7.0	13.1	11.5	1.87	1.64
1975	8.5	7.8	13.9	12.2	1.78	1.56
1974	5.6	5.0	9.9	8.1	1.98	1.62
1973	4.9	4.3	8.9	7.5	2.07	1.74
1972	5.6	5.0	10.4	—	2.08	—
1971	5.9	5.4	9.9	—	1.83	—
1970	4.9	4.5	8.2	—	1.82	—

Sources: U.S. Department of Labor, Bureau of Labor Statistics, *Employment in Perspective: Minority Workers*, no. 717, 1984; no. 737, 1986; no. 748, 1987; no. 764, 1988, for data from 1982 to 1986; *Monthly Labor Review* 110(October 1987): 69; U.S. Department of Commerce, Bureau of the Census, *Statistical Abstract of the U.S.*, 1970-1980.

75

differential between these two minority groups has consistently exceeded 3 per cent. The percentage of unemployed Hispanics also declined from 1983 to 1988. The 1988 rate of 8.2 per cent was 3.5 percentage points lower than the rate for black workers.

Since 1977, the black/white ratio has exceeded 2.0 in every year drifting upwards to 2.45. The Hispanic/white ratio has never reached 2.0 and has remained relatively stable ranging between 1.56 and 1.77 since 1977.

Female/Male Unemployment Differential. From the post World War II period until 1982, women's rate of unemployment exceeded men's by several percentage points. During the current decade, these differences have diminished. In 1987, men and women had the same rate of unemployment. As the statistics in Table 5.5 indicate, while there are variations between the sexes from year to year, since 1981 these fluctuations have been relatively small. During the period between 1982 and 1983, the sex ratio was less than one. This switch can be partly attributed to the fact that the industries in which women are employed, such as services and government, are less likely to be affected by business downturns than the goods producing industries that men dominate. Secondly, in that women's attachment to the work force is weaker than men's, they are more likely to exit from the labor market when jobs are scarce and the possibilities for finding work are discouraging.[74] Presently, there is little apparent difference between the sexes in their rate of unemployment, but changes in the labor market could alter this situation. An important exception to this general pattern is the relatively high rate of unemployment experienced by

TABLE 5.5

Unemployment Rates Among Civilian Men and Women: 1970-1988

	1970	1975	1980	1981	1982	1983	1984	1985	1986	1987	1988
M%	4.4	7.9	6.9	7.4	9.9	9.9	7.4	7.0	6.9	6.2	5.5
F%	5.9	9.3	7.4	7.9	9.4	9.2	7.6	7.4	7.1	6.2	5.6
F/M	1.34	1.17	1.18	1.07	.95	.93	1.03	1.06	1.03	1.0	1.0
FHead%[a]	5.6	10.1	9.0	9.9	11.1	14.2	11.3	10.4	9.8	9.2	8.1

[a]FHead = Female head of household.
Sources: U.S. Department of Labor, Bureau of Labor Statistics, *Handbook of Labor Statistics*, 1985; *Monthly Labor Review* (September 1987): 93; BLS, *Employment in Perspective: Minority Workers*, nos. 748 and 749, 1987; 764, 1988; U.S. Department of Commerce, Bureau of the Census, *Statistical Abstract of the U.S.*, 1970-1987.

women who maintain households. Among this group unemployment increased from 1975 onward and equaled or exceeded 9 per cent through 1987. In 1988 the unemployment level decreased to 8.1 per cent.

The changing industrial structure has played a key role in this shift in the unemployment differential. On the one hand, employment levels in male-dominated manufacturing industries have declined while on the other hand, women have taken advantage of the new jobs offered in the service sector. At the same time, women have begun to penetrate a greater range of industries enhancing their employment prospects. For example, the proportion of women in mining, manufacturing, and transportation has grown by more than an average of 1 per cent each year since 1964. In manufacturing, women increased their share of jobs from 26 per cent in 1964 to 32 per cent by 1982. The pattern of growth in these industries, as well as the extent to which certain industries continue to be dominated by members of one sex will have a substantial impact on the future unemployment differential between the sexes.[75]

Disabled Workers. According to the 1980 U.S. Census, 12.9 million Americans between the ages of 16 and 64 reported having a disability that limits the amount or kind of work they can perform or totally prevents them from working. This group represents approximately 8.5 per cent of Americans of working age, or slightly more than one in twelve persons.[76] These figures are low in comparison to those for persons above the age of 64. Figure 5.A reveals an association between disabilities and advancing age. Of the older adult population those reporting a work disability represent 22 per cent of all individuals ages 55 to 64; 32 per cent of those in ages 65 to 74, and 49 per cent of those age 75 and older.

While age is the most significant demographic variable associated with disability, those with less education appear to have a higher incidence of self-reported disability than those with more education. Most disabled workers are not actively looking for work, nor participating in work activities. When viewed by sex, disabled men are more likely to be employed than women.

Disabled persons work less than the nondisabled and earn less when they do work. According to a private survey of the disabled population in 1986, about one-third are members of the work force. Studies have observed a decline in labor force participation from preceding decades.[77] The working disabled are concentrated in low-status occupations and are subject to some labor market discrimination. By their own report, one in four disabled persons experienced job discrimination in their current position. [78]

As the data in Table 5.6 indicate, during the current decade the great majority of disabled persons are not participating in the work force. Men are more likely than women to be in the labor force and to hold full-time jobs.

FIGURE 5.A Adult Population by Age in 1980

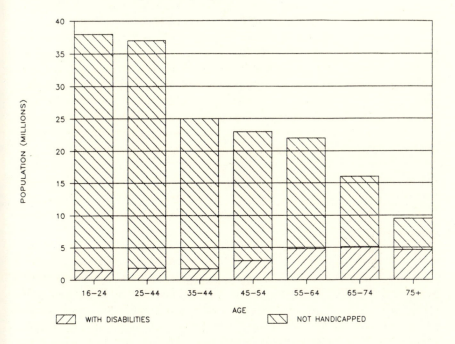

Source: U.S. National Council on the Handicapped, *Toward Independence*, 1986, 5.

About one-fourth of disabled men are full-time workers. In contrast, only one-fourth of all disabled women are in the work force, and about 11 per cent of women who have a disability hold a full-time job. Unemployment levels have been high for the disabled during this decade but are not sharply different by sex. While unemployment rates appear stable, the declining labor force participation of disabled men may be indicative of discouragement.

Veterans. Military veterans form a special class with respect to their rate of labor force participation and are a target group in many federal employment programs. Persons who served during the Vietnam conflict are more likely to be unemployed or out of the work force than others. This is partly due to their relatively high rate (14 per cent) of disability.[79] In 1970, 6.6 per cent of American men (20-34 years of age) who served during the Vietnam War were jobless. In comparison, 3.5 per cent of all men 20 years and over were unemployed in 1970. In 1975 veterans' rate of unemployment was 9.9 per cent which was 2.6 percentage points higher than the rate

TABLE 5.6

Employment Status of Disabled Americans by Sex: 1981 and 1985

Status		1981 Male	Female	1985 Male	Female
In Labor Force	%	41.5	23.7	37.3	25.0
Full-Time	%	27.4	11.9	24.3	11.3
Unemployed	%	16.9	18.3	16.4	17.0
Not in Labor Force	%	58.5	76.3	62.7	75.0

Source: U.S. Department of Commerce, Bureau of the Census, Statistical Abstract of the United States, 1985 and 1987.

for all adult males.[80] By 1987, the pattern of high unemployment could still be observed among Vietnam era veterans between 30 and 34 years of age where at 9.4 per cent unemployment exceeded the rate for non-veterans by 4.9 percentage points. In other age categories there were no large differences related to veteran status. There is evidence that this group of veterans has had higher than normal rates of unemployment in the preceding periods of 1980 and 1977, in that high rates of unemployment are apparent for the cohort in the lower age category, 25-29 years. The data are reported below in Table 5.7.

Displaced Workers. As a result of changes in the structure of the U.S. economy and economic recessions, a large group of workers who had previously enjoyed stable employment found their skills and experience in low demands. Slack work and closings affected 10.1 million American workers between 1981 and 1986. Of these, 5.1 million who had held their former jobs at least three years were classified as "displaced." In fact, the median years on the lost job for all displaced workers in this period was 6.6 years.[81]

Half of the persons displaced from their jobs between 1979 and 1986 had been employed in manufacturing; particularly heavy losses occurred in electrical and non-electrical machinery and primary metals. About 10 per cent of those displaced from their jobs came from service industries. Losses in the primary sector accounted for 1.6 per cent of displacement. In the public sector, 55,000 workers were displaced. Among occupational groups, the toll was heaviest among blue collar workers with 1.9 million out of work

TABLE 5.7

Unemployment Rates of Vietnam-Era Veterans

Status: Age:	Veteran 25-29	30-34	Non-Veteran 25-29	30-34
1987	(a)	9.4	6.3[b]	4.5
1980	9.9	5.1	7.5	5.4
1977	7.0	4.4	6.5	4.5
1970	4.3	3.3	3.8	3.1

[a] Too few in this age category to estimate in 1987
[b] Includes all males.
Sources: U.S. Department of Labor, Bureau of Labor Statistics, *Labor Force Statistics Derived from the Current Population Survey*, vol. 1, Table B11; BLS, *News*, 87-536, December 1987; unpublished data U.S. Department of Labor.

as a result of structural change. Geographically, the northern midwestern section of the country (Michigan, Illinois, Indiana, Ohio, and Wisconsin) had the highest concentration of displaced workers and came to be known as the nation's "rust belt." More than 1.1 million midwestern workers lost their jobs between 1981 and 1986. [82]

Displacement and reemployment affected demographic groups differently as seen in Table 5.8. Two-thirds of those displaced from jobs they had held at least three years were men. Reemployment rates were about 10 percentage points lower for minority workers than they have been for whites. Almost one-fourth of the displaced females left the work force, and the tendency was more common for women over 55 years of age. Similarly, while 10 per cent of all displaced males left the work force, more than one-third of those over 55 years of age exited. By 1986, 67 per cent of those who had lost their jobs during the period from 1981 to 1985 were reemployed. Less than one-fifth of this group remained jobless. This is an improvement over previous periods.

The impact of labor market practices is noteworthy. More than half of those whose jobs were terminated between 1981 and 1986 did receive advance notification of expected a layoff, but the majority did not leave before their job ended. One in three workers found a new job within five weeks of dismissal. About 3.4 million received unemployment benefits for some period, but 80 per cent were without any health insurance in January 1986. Finally, geographic mobility occurred among 14 per cent of those

TABLE 5.8

Employment Status of Displaced Workers[a] by Sex and Race,
January 1986

	N thousand	Re-employed %	Un-employed %	Not in labor force %
Total	5,130	66.9	17.8	15.3
Sex				
Male	3,321	70.9	18.6	10.5
Female	1,810	59.6	16.2	24.1
Race				
White	4,452	68.2	16.2	15.6
Black	581	57.7	29.2	13.1
Hispanic	311	56.6	27.2	16.1

[a]Persons with minimum job tenure of 3 years in job lost due to plant closings, movings, slack work, or redundancy.
Source: Francis W. Horvarth, "The Pulse of Economic Change: Displaced Workers of 1981-1985," Monthly Labor Review 107(June 1987): 12.

displaced, and those who did move were significantly more likely to become reemployed (82%) than those who remained behind (64%).[83]

Examining the displaced workers by industry, higher rates of reemployment are observed in construction, finance, and real estate. Persistent unemployment levels were highest for services, agriculture, and transportation workers. Evidence of discouragement is strongest among predominantly female retail trade workers where more than one in five left the work force after displacement from their previous job. Table 5.9 reports these data.

Americans who lost jobs in industries that failed to compete successfully with foreign goods producers generally do not have the necessary skills to obtain jobs in industries where exports are expanding. Industries adversely affected by trade tend to have employed minority group members with lower skills and less education. Thus the difficulties of relocating persons displaced from jobs in industries such as footwear and apparel is compounded by that fact that opportunities for employment in unskilled jobs have diminished.[84]

Discouraged Workers. In that they may hide the true level of unemployment, discouraged workers (people who want a job and are able to take one but are not looking for work because they think they cannot find a job) must also be counted. Individuals who terminate their efforts to participate in the labor force form a group of "discouraged workers" who are among the 5.7 million people who said they wanted a job but were not actively seeking one. About one-fourth of these discouraged workers are persons who instead of participating in the work force are keeping busy with housework, as shown in Table 5.10. This group is predominantly female.

TABLE 5.9

Displaced Workers'[a] Employment Status by Industry of Lost Job, January 1986

Industry	Number thousands	Re-employed	Unem-ployed	Not in labor force
Non-Agricultural				
wage and salary	4,772	67.2	17.6	15.2
Mining	175	67.4	17.4	15.2
Construction	316	74.8	16.6	8.6
Manufacturing	2,550	65.9	18.2	15.9
Transportation &				
Public Utilities	386	66.9	20.0	13.1
Wholesale & Retail				
Trade	689	66.3	12.4	21.3
Finance Insurance &				
Real Estate	107	73.5	12.5	14.0
Services	540	68.4	21.4	10.2
Agricultural Wage and				
Salary workers	141	66.0	20.9	13.1
Government	172	63.0	18.9	18.0
Self-Employment	33	(b)	(b)	(b)

[a]Persons with minimum job tenure of 3 years in job lost due to plant closings, moving, slack work, or redundancy.
[b] Estimates unreliable.
Source: Francis W. Horvarth, "The Pulse of Economic Change: Displaced Workers of 1981-1985," *Monthly Labor Review* 107(June 1987): 12.

The proportion citing this reason has decreased slightly over time. In 1987, 18 per cent of those not seeking a job reported they felt they could not find one. This proportion represents a slight decline from 1985. The volume of persons indicating they do not want to work has not declined over time. In fact, since 1980 eight million more individuals are in this category, slightly less than half of these people report they are occupied by keeping house. This proportion has declined from almost two-thirds in 1970, as seen in Table 5.10. Women's linkage to the work force is not as strong as men's in the United States. As noted above, among displaced workers, women are much more likely than men to exit from the work force after losing their previous job.

TABLE 5.10

Persons Not in the Labor Force by Job Desire and Reason for Not Seeking Work, 1970 to 1987

Reason Not in Labor Force	1970	1975	1980	1985	1986	1987
Do not want a job (millions)	50.4	54.1	55.1	56.8	56.9	62.9
per cent keeping house	63.8	58.5	53.1	47.8	46.3	45.0
Want a job but						
not looking (millions)[a]	3.9	5.3	6.5	5.9	5.8	5.7
per cent: in school	27.7	27.7	26.6	24.5	24.4	24.9
ill/disabled	12.6	12.9	13.3	13.5	14.5	15.1
keeping house	23.4	21.3	22.3	22.2	22.4	22.2
think cannot get a job (discouraged workers)	16.5	20.7	17.5	20.3	19.7	18.0

[a]Includes reasons for not looking that are not shown separately.
Source: U.S. Department of Commerce, Bureau of the Census, Statistical Abstract of the U.S., 1987, Table 647.

Only a small portion of discouraged American workers never held jobs (less than 16 per cent between 1979 and 1986). Job market factors are cited by about two-thirds of all discouraged workers (see Table 5.11). Personal reasons are consistently less frequently claimed by both sexes. During recessionary periods, job market factors were cited more often in the United States. With the exception of this cyclical trend, the patterns observed in the USA are not unique.[85]

The ranks of jobless persons indicating that they wanted a job and were able to take one grew during the 1970s, peaking in the early 1980s and then tapering off in 1985 when 1.2 million Americans were discouraged from looking for work. Economic cycles are clearly contributory.

TABLE 5.11

Discouraged U.S. Workers by Reason, Sex, and Year

	Job Market Reasons			Personal Reasons		
	All	Male	Female	All	Male	Female
1986	69.5	70.5	68.4	30.8	29.5	31.6
1985	68.1	68.7	67.8	31.9	31.3	32.2
1983	76.1	77.1	75.4	23.9	22.9	24.6
1982	75.3	76.5	74.5	24.7	23.5	25.5
1970	66.7	63.8	68.0	33.3	36.2	32.0

Source: OECD, Employment Outlook, 1987, 144.

During the period between 1970 and 1987, the proportion of discouraged workers among unemployed workers was highest in 1970 at 15.6 per cent and in 1983 at 15.3 per cent. Since 1983, the proportion declined reaching 13.7 per cent in 1986. According to OECD estimations, the ratio of discouraged to unemployed workers is relatively modest. Historically, the proportion of women who have been discouraged from job seeking activities is higher than the rate for men.[86] The data are presented in Table 5.12. Among racial and ethnic groups more than two-thirds of discouraged workers in 1987 were white (68%); blacks represented 29 per cent of discouraged workers; and 10 per cent of Hispanics (who are included in both black and white racial groups) were discouraged from looking for work. Relative to their share of the U.S. population, whites (86%) were underrepresented, Hispanics (7%) were overrepresented, and blacks (11%) were largely overrepresented among the ranks of the discouraged.

Non Full-time Workers. Part-time, part-year, and temporary workers can be distinguished from full-time employees in the United States by their disadvantageous employment status. In addition to lower wages and fewer fringe benefits, persons who are not permanent full-time employees tend to have higher rates of unemployment than others. They are expendable employees who are shed relatively quickly when the demand for labor slackens. Employers are slower to re-hire these contingent workers during recovery periods than they are to discharge them during

TABLE 5.12

Discouraged Workers as a Percentage of Unemployed Workers by Sex and Year

	All	Male	Female
1987	13.8	10.4	18.1
1986	13.7	9.7	18.5
1985	14.5	11.2	18.4
1984	15.1	10.3	20.9
1983	15.3	10.4	22.2
1982	14.7	9.5	21.8
1979	12.6	9.2	16.0
1976	12.5	8.1	17.8
1970	15.6	9.9	22.5

Sources: OECD, *Employment Outlook*, 1987; U.S. Department of Labor, Bureau of Labor Statistics, *Employment in Perspective: Minority Workers*, no. 748, 1987.

downturns. Little data are available regarding the unemployment patterns of temporary workers, but information regarding part-time employees is insightful. As the data reported in Table 5.13 indicate, the ratio of unemployment for part time workers relative to those holding full time jobs was close to unity in 1982 and 1983, but since the recovery from the last recession, part-time workers have experienced much greater rates of unemployment than those holding full-time jobs. For the last three years, 1984 to 1987, the ratio has equaled 1.4. When persons working year round are compared to those holding part-year jobs the disparity is substantial. According to data from the Current Population Survey, more than 90 per cent of those employed part of a year experience unemployment.

5.2 The Geographic Distribution of Unemployment

Unemployment rates vary considerably across the United States. Civilian unemployment levels for the states are estimated from the Current Population Survey. Historically, high rates of unemployment have plagued certain states. These include the Appalachian mountain states of Kentucky, West Virginia, and Tennessee and the southern states of Louisiana, Mississippi, and Alabama. Unemployment has also been high in Alaska as a result of over-immigration motivated by the discovery of oil and subsequent construction of the Alaskan oil-pipeline during the 1970s. Figure 5.B shows the average rates of unemployment by state for 1987.

TABLE 5.13

Unemployment Rates of Part-Time and Full-Time Employees, 1970-1987

	1970	1975	1980	1981	1982	1983	1984	1985	1986	1987
Full-time	4.5	8.1	6.8	7.3	9.6	9.5	7.2	6.8	6.6	5.8
Part-time	7.6	10.3	8.7	9.4	10.5	10.4	9.3	9.3	9.1	8.4
Ratio— PT/FT	1.7	1.3	1.3	1.3	1.1	1.1	1.3	1.4	1.4	1.4

Sources: U.S. Department of Labor, Bureau of Labor Statistics, *Handbook of Labor Statistics*, 1985, Table 48; *Monthly Labor Review*, various issues, 1985-1988.

In 1987, when the national unemployment rate was 6.2 per cent, four states had unemployment levels equal to or above 10 per cent. Fourteen states had unemployment rates below 5 per cent, twice as many as in 1986. States with the highest levels of unemployment were generally located in the central part of the country where manufacturing is a dominant feature of the labor market. Beyond the continental United States, Alaska experienced an unemployment rate of 10.8 per cent and the territory of Puerto Rico recorded 16.8 per cent unemployed, which was a decrease of almost 2.1 per cent from the 1986 estimate. Unemployment in the State of Hawaii was estimated at 3.8 per cent.

Regional unemployment patterns are reported in Table 5.14. The rate of civilian unemployment declined in 44 states and the nation's capital, Washington, D.C., between 1986 and 1987. In comparison with the recessionary year of 1983, more dispersion in the geographic pattern of unemployment is evident. The regional economies of the United States appear to be becoming more diversified than they were in the past with a somewhat more even distribution of manufacturing and less sensitivity to cyclical trends in particular industries.

A clear reordering of the regions with respect to relative rates of unemployment is evident in the data reported in Table 5.14. In 1973, the lowest levels of unemployment were found among the southern states and the highest unemployment rates occurred in the western region of the U.S. By 1983, the northeast had the lowest regional level of unemployment and this has remained so through 1987. Since 1986, the highest regional unemployment rate is found in the southern states.

86

FIGURE 5.B Unemployment by State, 1987 Annual Averages

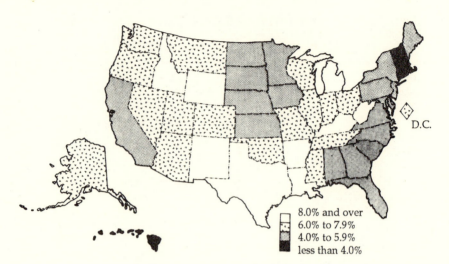

8.0% and over
6.0% to 7.9%
4.0% to 5.9%
less than 4.0%

Source: U.S. Department of Labor, Bureau of Labor Statistics, *News*, 88-76, Feb. 1988.

5.3 The Duration of Unemployment and Insurance Benefits

There has been notable spread in the duration of unemployment in the United States over the current decade. The shortest average period to date was observed in 1980 at 11.9 weeks, the longest in 1982 at 20 weeks. In fact, the duration of unemployment recorded for 1982 and 1984 was higher than any other years within the time span between 1960 and 1986. Since 1975, the average annual duration of unemployment has consistently exceeded ten weeks. In 1987, the average unemployment period was 14.5 weeks. It declined to an average of 13.5 weeks in 1988. Table 5.15 reports statistics pertaining to unemployment duration and benefit coverage from 1960 to 1988.

While the largest share of unemployment is consistently less than five weeks, the proportion out of work for 27 weeks or more has generally been higher during the 1980s than in the preceding decade. For most years, the average insured period of benefits exceeded the average length of unemployment. But between one-fifth and one-third of the unemployed exhausted their unemployment insurance each year. The highest rates of uninsured unemployment for members of the unemployment trust fund were observed in the mid-1970s and the early 1980s when one-third or more of the beneficiaries were not able to find a job before their benefits expired. In actual numbers, about 4.2 million individuals exhausted the regular

TABLE 5.14

Regional Unemployment Rate in the U.S., Selected Years

	1973	1975	1979	1983	1985	1986	1987
Total U.S.	4.9	8.5	5.8	9.6	7.2	7.0	6.2
Northeast	5.5	9.5	6.6	8.7	6.2	5.6	4.5
North Central	4.4	7.9	5.5	10.8	8.0	7.3	6.7
South	4.1	7.7	5.4	9.3	7.2	7.6	6.8
West	6.5	9.2	6.0	9.5	7.3	7.1	6.3

Source: U.S. Department of Labor, Bureau of Labor Statistics, *News*, 88-76, February 1988.

unemployment benefits in 1975, 1982, and 1983. In 1984 and 1985, about 2.6 million unemployed individuals exhausted their regular insurance benefits. Of the persons receiving extended benefits, the largest number of exhaustions occurred in 1976. In the early 1980s the rate was highest in 1982 at 1.2 million cases, but by 1984 only 50,000 people were in this situation.[87] Despite the decline in the rate and volume of unemployment occurring in 1987, the proportion of unemployed persons who were without work for 15 weeks or more was essentially unchanged from 1985 to 1987.

Scope of Unemployment Coverage. Not all American workers are eligible for unemployment insurance, although the great majority of jobs are covered by the program. As Table 5.15 indicates, the proportion of unemployed workers receiving unemployment insurance (UI) benefits has ranged between 50 and 29 per cent of the work force during the period between 1970 and 1986. The proportion of workers receiving UI benefits during the 1980s has generally been lower than during other periods. An individual's recent employment history including length of employment and previous earnings are criteria for eligibility which is established by the states. New entrants and most re-entrants into the work force are ineligible for coverage. Discouraged workers, low wage earners and those involuntarily employed part-time have little likelihood of receiving state UI benefits, but the latter represent about one in six of those who are recipients of supplemental unemployment benefits.[88]

An individual can become disqualified by failing to apply for employment with a state employment service office or by refusing to accept a job

88

TABLE 5.15

Insured Unemployment, 1960 - 1988

Year	Insured as a percentage of total Unemployed	Per cent of Insured Workers who were Unemployed	Average Duration in Weeks	Average Duration of Benefits in weeks for all Claims	for Exhaustees	Initial Claimants Exhausting Regular Benefits %
1988	32[a]	2.1[a]	13.5[a]	13.3[a]	——	——
1987	32	2.4	14.5	14.0	——	——
1986	32	2.8	15.0	14.6	22.7	32.5
1985	31	2.9	15.6	14.3	22.6	31.3
1984	29	2.8	18.2	14.4	23.1	33.5
1983	32	3.9	15.6	17.5	23.6	38.4
1982	38	4.6	20.0	15.9	22.6	38.5
1981	37	6.0	13.7	14.5	22.8	32.4
1980	44	3.9	11.9	14.9	22.8	33.2
1979	40	2.9	10.9	13.1	21.5	26.7
1978	38	3.3	11.9	13.3	22.5	26.8
1977	38	3.9	14.3	14.2	22.1	33.4
1976	40	4.6	15.8	14.9	21.2	37.8
1975	50	6.0	14.1	15.7	21.2	37.8
1974	44	3.5	9.7	12.7	22.4	31.2
1973	37	2.7	10.0	13.4	22.5	27.6
1972	38	3.5	12.1	14.2	22.7	28.9
1971	43	4.1	11.4	14.4	22.7	30.5
1970	44	3.4	8.8	12.3	22.1	24.4
1969	39	2.1	7.9	11.4	21.4	19.8
1965	39	3.0	11.8	12.2	21.3	21.5
1960	49	4.8	12.8	12.7	21.4	26.1

[a]Estimates.
Sources: U.S. Department of Labor, Employment and Training Administration, *Employment and Training Handbook* and supplementary tables, 1986 and 1987; Unpublished data from the Unemployment Insurance System; U.S. Congress, House, Committee on Government Operations, *Changes in the Unemployment Insurance System: Is the Safety Net Eroding?*, 99th Cong., 2d sess., 22 May 1986. Other computations made from BLS, *Handbook of Labor Statistics*, June 1985; U.S. Congress, House, Committee on Ways and Means, *Background Material and Data on Programs within the Jurisdiction of the Committee*, 101st Cong., 2d sess., 15 March 1989.

---

for which he or she is considered to be appropriate. Persons who lost their last job due to misconduct are ineligible for coverage. Variations exist among the states in the proportion of persons ruled ineligible due to charges of misconduct from their former employer. In 1985, 7.7 per cent of jobless Nebraskans were denied benefits for this cause but only 1.1 per cent of the workers in the State of Maine were ruled ineligible for misconduct. In eight states, more than 5.0 per cent of the unemployed did not receive UI benefits because of misconduct charges. The median rate of denial was 2.72 per cent in 1985.[89]

TABLE 5.16

Distribution of Unemployment by Duration in Weeks from 1977 to 1987

Period	Less than 5 weeks	5-14 weeks	15-26 weeks	27 and more wks.	Total[a]
Year	%	%	%	%	%
1987	44	30	13	14	101
1986	42	31	13	14	99
1985	42	30	12	15	99
1984	39	29	13	19	100
1983	33	27	15	24	99
1982	36	31	16	17	100
1981	42	31	14	14	101
1980	43	32	14	11	100
1979	48	32	12	9	101
1978	46	31	12	10	99
1977	42	31	13	15	101

[a]Totals may not add to 100% due to rounding.
Sources: U.S. Congress, House, Committee on Ways and Means, Background Material and Data on Programs within the Jurisdiction of the Committee, 100th Cong., 1st sess., 6 March 1987; Monthly Labor Review 111(February 1988): 90.

Of those whose earnings are insured, the rate of unemployment is substantially lower than the rate of unemployment in the work force at-large. The yearly proportion of the insured work force that was jobless is shown in Table 5.15. These figures did not exceed 6.0 per cent for the studied period. During the current decade, the proportion of jobless insured workers has declined from the relatively high level of 6 per cent in 1981 to 2.1 per cent in 1988. The data are graphically portrayed in Figure 5.C.

As Table 5.17 shows, the ratio of insured to uninsured unemployment has been lower in the 1980s than in preceding periods and declined by 17 per cent between 1980 and 1986. Some speculate that stricter eligibility rules imposed by the States may account for this decrease in eligibility for coverage,[90] but other factors including greater fluidity in and out of the ranks of unemployment and an increase in the number of peripheral workers may also reduce the proportion of the work force able to meet eligibility standards.

TABLE 5.17

Ratio of Insured to Uninsured Unemployment, 1975-1986

1975	1976	1977	1978	1979	1980	1981	1982	1983	1984	1985	1986
.76	.67	.56	.43	.42	.50	.41	.45	.44	.34	.34	.33

Source: U.S. Congress, House, Committee on Ways and Means, Background Material and Data on Programs within the Jurisdiction of the Committee, 100th Cong., 1st sess., 6 March 1987.

Although the rate of unemployment is presently low by American standards, the extent to which American workers are in jeopardy from unemployment appears to have increased during the 1980s. Three factors lead to this conclusion. First, as indicated in Table 5.15, the average duration of unemployment during the current decade is higher than it has been in past periods. A second factor is that during the 1980s the proportion of workers who have exhausted their unemployment insurance benefits has exceeded 30 per cent in each year. The third factor increasing the risk a worker incurs is that since 1983 less than one-third of the jobless could draw upon unemployment insurance compared with a rate of 50 per cent in 1975. Finally, although the rate of income replacement has been fairly constant, unemployment benefits received from 1987 onward are subject to federal income tax.

5.4 Summary

This chapter provides information about the pattern of unemployment and the current trend toward lower rates of joblessness in the United States. The principal findings are listed here.

FIGURE 5.C

Proportion of Unemployed Workers Receiving Unemployment Insurance

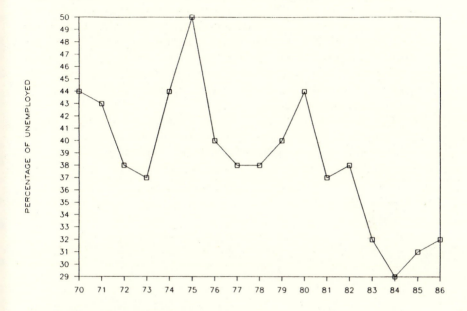

Source: Data reported in Table 5.15.

• Between 1982 and 1987 unemployment declined by 3.4 per cent.
• Job losers have consistently been the largest group of unemployed persons, but their share of unemployment declined from 59 per cent in 1982 to 47 per cent in 1987. The second largest group is made up of persons trying to re-enter the labor market. About one-fourth of the jobless are in this position.
• Among demographic group, whites have the lowest rates of job lessness but a steady decline in unemployment is apparent among His panics. Black unemployment patterns are more unique and the rate is substantially greater than white or Hispanic levels.
• Similarly among youth, the disparity between white and other teens is striking, but there has been a decline in this unemployment differential in recent years.
• Between males and females a historical unemployment differential has dissolved, but female heads of households remain at a greater dis advantage in securing work.
• About two thirds of displaced workers re-enter the work force;

- About two thirds of displaced workers re-enter the work force; those who exit are disproportionately female.
- The number of persons who do not want a job increased sharply between 1985/86 and 1987. Of those who want a job but have stopped looking, one-fourth are in school and 22 per cent are keeping house. Discouraged workers accounted for 18 per cent of those not seeking work who wanted a job.
- Regional shifts in the pattern of unemployment have occurred with relatively fewer jobless in the Northeast and more unemployed in the South and North Central regions.
- During the 1980s the average weeks of unemployment experienced by individual workers has been higher than in previous periods. The proportion of initial claimants exhausting their insurance benefits exceeded 30 per cent during this decade while the proportion of jobless workers eligible for unemployment has generally declined.

6
Outcome of Labor Market Policy and the Policy Process

6.1 Introduction

Although the United States has lagged in the development of labor market policy and the refinement of instruments and mechanisms to affect changes in the supply and demand for labor, considerable effort has been focused in this country on methods for assessing the outcomes of employment policies and programs. In this chapter, the national experience with job training and job creation programs is described and assessments of program effectiveness from program evaluations are presented.

Labor market policy initiatives in the United States have evolved toward a cooperative relationship between the public and private sectors in both training and job opportunities. This shared responsibility is in keeping with current public opinion as well as political reality. In the absence of a coordinated policy process, integrated program activities, and centralized administration of labor market measures there is less advantage for government to control the production of job creation and training activities.

6.2 Labor Market Training Programs

A thin trail of job training programs can be traced back to the early 1900s, but in the U.S. active employment training programs, like so many other social programs, came of age in the 1960s. An exception is the Vocational Rehabilitation Act which provides subsidies for training and rehabilitation. In 1955, 200,000 persons were served at a cost per client of about $830. Until 1980, the Vocational Rehabilitation Act steadily expanded its clientele along with its fiscal resources.

The 1960s: Promulgation of Training Programs. In the early 1960s, two important programs were enacted to provide employment training. Under the Area Redevelopment Act of 1961, the precedent of paying cash allowances to workers in training courses was established. The Act, which was vetoed by President Eisenhower but signed into law by John F. Kennedy, provided that persons in designated economically distressed regions could receive benefits for a maximum of 16 weeks.

In the following year (1962), the more substantial Manpower Development and Training Act (MDTA) was passed. Many cite the event as the initiation of active labor market policy in the United States. The initial appropriation entailed one-half billion dollars for three years. It provided for vocational education in both classroom and on-the-job settings. Under MDTA, costs for tuition, transportation, and living were paid for a maximum of two years. While the original intent of the legislation was to enhance the quality of the labor force to match the demand for more specialized workers by upgrading skills and retraining workers whose skills had become obsolete because of automation, the focus shifted to job training for economically disadvantaged workers. By 1973, only one-third of MDTA trainees were selected on the basis of labor market needs.[91]

Two programs from the 1960s that target the economically disadvantaged have been extended into the 1980s. One is the Job Corps which was established in 1964 under the Economic Opportunity Act (PL 88-452). Its unique feature is that it removes trainees from their environment and houses them collectively with the intent of breaking the pattern of negative reinforcement from their environment. Later, in 1967, the Work Incentive Program (WIN) which targets welfare recipients for training and job counseling was established. This is the only U.S. program aimed directly at welfare recipients. At the national level both the Departments of Labor and Health and Human Services administer the program.

Training programs for special occupational fields, particularly persons in the transportation industry, have been provided for under a variety of federal entitlements including the Urban Mass Transportation Act (PL 89-365) which served as a model for subsequent legislation; the Demonstration Cities Act of 1966 (PL 89-754); and the Rail Passenger Services Act of 1970 (PL 91-518). Training opportunities for workers displaced from their jobs as a result of federal deinstitutionalization policy were also offered under mandates providing for the release of the institutionalized (PL 93-200; PL 95-602; PL 94-63).

Because it provided para-professional and technical skills, the training component of the New Careers program is distinct from other American training schemes. The program, which along with the Job Corps was enacted in 1964, offered training to economically disadvantaged persons in occupations such as legal assistant, health technician, and teaching assistant. Participants were closely screened and the New Careers programs was relatively small.

The 1970s: Consolidation. Early in the 1970s, the various employment programs were consolidated under the Comprehensive Employment and Training Act of 1973 (CETA) (PL93-203). During this decade, no major programs for job training were initiated. There were, however, provisions for training specific groups of people under various entitlements. Training for displaced rail workers was included in the Rail Passenger Service Act of 1970 (PL 91-518) and for institutional workers affected by federal deinstitutionalization policies under other laws (PL 93-415; PL 94-63; PL 95-602).

Under the Trade Adjustment Act of 1974, federal funds were allotted for workers in industries affected by U.S. trade policies. These funds have amounted to about $30 million each year in the latter half of the 1980s, but during the 1970s the highest annual allocation was $12 million (1978, 1979). In 1977, Help through Industry Retraining was initiated with the mandate of providing training for disabled and disadvantaged Vietnam veterans. The Skill Training Improvement Program aimed at providing highly skilled training to workers was implemented in the same year.

CETA shifted program development responsibilities to the local level of government using block grants instead of more restrictive categorical grants as the funding mechanism. However, expenditures were audited by the U.S. Department of Labor to assure that funds were used within the provisions of the legislation. Four hundred local government units were responsible for coordinating training initiatives under CETA.

Funding to the states was distributed according to a formula based on a jurisdiction's previous funding level, unemployment rate, and poverty levels. Much of the money was used to create temporary jobs in state and local government and in nonprofit organizations. Originally, the primary goal of CETA was to provide training for disadvantaged workers, but the focus shifted with the economic situation. During the recessionary years of 1974 and 1975, the emphasis was on providing employment in the public sector. In 1978, the focus was on controlling structural unemployment by providing assistance to only the most disadvantaged and hard-to-place. Finally, the focus shifted to providing training alone rather than public jobs.

During the 1970s, the precedent of providing special training assistance to women was established. Amendments passed in 1976 to the Federal Vocational Education Act extended funding to women who had been displaced from careers in the home because of widowhood, divorce, or the disability of their spouse. In 1978, under amendments to the Comprehensive Employment and Training Act, displaced homemakers were designated as a target population for federal assistance.

The 1980s: Retrenchment through Cutbacks and Privitization. The passage of the bipartisan Job Training Partnership Act (JTPA) (Public Law 97-300) in 1982 marks a clear shift in the orientation toward job training in the United States. The JTPA is distinguished by its emphasis on community involvement and decentralized administration. Within each state, geographic areas are designated (SDA) and Private Industry Councils (PIC) are formed to work with elected local officials in developing and overseeing a program to deliver appropriate job training skills to eligible residents.

The inclusion of representatives from industry in policy making and execution reflects the assumption that they will provide special insight into the type of programs needed to maximize the match between labor's skills and industry's needs. This point is central in that JTPA does not provide for job creation or employment within the public sector, unlike its predecessor, CETA. The idea of a public-private sector partnership was not unique to JTPA. In the late 1960s the federal government initiated several programs to form a cooperative relationship with the private sector that would produce jobs for disadvantaged and jobless persons. One major program from this period was called Job Opportunities in the Business Sector (JOBS). The National Alliance of Businessmen (NAB) worked in conjunction with the U.S. Department of Labor to hire and train on-the-job the hard-core unemployed. Training costs were absorbed by some businesses while others received partial reimbursement from the federal government.

The private sector orientation of JTPA leaves it open to criticisms that it serves business at the expense of labor. One charge is that employers are able to subsidize the cost of their normal training requirements with public funds. Another criticism is that the partnership between business and state governments excludes representatives from organized labor and local citizens.

6.3 Job Creation Activities

The pervasive American belief that unemployment represents a personal shortcoming was challenged in the 1930s during the Great Depression. Estimates of unemployment in 1933 were as high as one-third of the work force and many of those who did have jobs were paid substantially less than they had previously earned. In response to the extraordinary conditions, the administration of Franklin D. Roosevelt introduced the

"New Deal" program during this period. A principal component of the program was job creation in the public sector. Under the mandate of the New Deal, a wide variety of job creation measures were implemented by the U.S. Department of Labor, which provided millions of jobs. The Civilian Conservation Corps recruited about two million unmarried young men between 1933 and 1939 to work in the nation's forests and parks. About four million temporary jobs were created under the Civil Works administration and another eight million men were employed under the Works Progress Administration.

The job creation programs sponsored by the government under the New Deal were terminated during the 1940s when World War II enlistments sharply reduced the rate of unemployment. Many attempts to launch job creation programs were made during the 1960s as part of the war on poverty. The primary emphasis of these programs was to provide training and work experience for persons classified as economically disadvantaged. Job creation activities were undertaken by four different public programs during this period. These were the Neighborhood Youth Corps (NYC) which provided jobs for teenagers so they could complete their schooling; Operation Mainstream which offered workers over 55 years of age non profit and public jobs in community improvement and service delivery; Public Service Careers which located jobs in government and nonprofit agencies for skilled workers; and the National Association of Businessmen-Job Opportunities in the Business Sector which was a private sector program that sought to find jobs in business and industry for disadvantaged persons. All of these programs were modest in scale. Of the jobs programs launched during this period, the Job Corps, which was renewed under the Job Training Partnership Act, has been the most enduring.

In the early 1970s, many U.S. employment programs were consolidated under the Comprehensive Employment and Training Act (CETA). The legislation provided a vehicle to carry a number of employment creation programs into the 1970s. Programs designed to alleviate youth joblessness that were authorized under the CETA legislation included the Summer Youth Employment Program, Youth Community Conservation and Improvement Projects, and the Young Adult Conservation Corps.

In 1971, with the passage of the Emergency Employment Act, the Public Service Employment (PSE) program was established as a countercyclical measure in response to high rates of unemployment. This program was incorporated into the CETA legislation in 1973. The inclusion of the Public Service Employment (PSE) was originally secondary to training activities under CETA but became increasingly important over time. From the implementation of the CETA legislation until 1977, enrollment in public service employment programs doubled. Legislative amendments to CETA in 1974 and 1978 expanded the PSE program. An amendment also added another countercyclical program initiated in the 1970s, the Emergency Jobs and Unemployment Assistance Act of 1974. This program, which was added to CETA under Title VI, is discussed ahead.

Beneficiaries under job creation programs funded by CETA IID and VI peaked in 1978 and 1979 with more than one million persons in publicly-funded jobs in each of those years. In 1980, the number of beneficiaries declined to about 847,000 persons. Similarly, job creation program expenditures exceeded five billion dollars in 1978 and 1979. The data are reported in Table 6.1.

Also affecting the demand structure during this period was the passage of the New Jobs Tax Credit Program in 1977 which enabled employers to deduct a 50 per cent credit from their tax obligation for up to 6,000 paid in wages. A similar incentive known as the Targeted Jobs Tax Credit was aimed at veterans and disadvantaged workers. Both required that employers exceed their previous annual employment levels by 102 per cent. Similarly, the provision of a retroactive investment tax credit to steel producers under the Tax Reform Act of 1986 (section 212) provided an economic stimulus to stabilize the steel industry and limit further decline in employment levels.[92]

TABLE 6.1

Job Creation Expenditures and Benificiaries Under CETA IID and VI, 1975 to 1980

	1975	1976	TQ1976[a]	1977	1978	1979	1980
$ Millions	838.4	2416.4	596.9	2836.4	5764.2	5023.4	3634.6
Beneficiaries hundreds	366.8	584.9	382.1	783.3	1,207.0	1,105.2	847.3

[a]TQ= Transitional Quarter.
Source: U.S. General Accounting Office, CETA Programs for Disadvantaged Adults, June 1982.

In response to the eleven-month economic recession of 1960-1961, countercylical efforts were initiated to combat an unemployment rate of 6.9 per cent. These included the Accelerated Public Works Program and two Local Public Works Programs. Job Creation activities accelerated in the U.S. during the 1970s. The passage of the Emergency Employment Act of 1971 marks the beginning of this cycle. This was the first major job creation program initiated in the U.S. since the New Deal. The Public Employment Program which was authorized under this legislation was designed to serve as an escape valve for high rates of unemployment. When unemployment increased, temporary jobs would be created in government to absorb those who would otherwise flow into the ranks of the unemployed. The program selected as its special targets veterans, those over 45, immigrants, displaced workers, disadvantaged workers, and poor families. The two-year program was appropriated $1 billion in 1972 and $1.25 billion in 1973. An average of 128,000 persons received payments each year. [93]

The Emergency Jobs and Unemployment Assistance Act (PL93-567) was passed in 1974, adding Title VI to the CETA legislation. This was a temporary jobs program in response to the 1973-1975 recession for persons who had been jobless for one month or longer. Under Title VI of CETA the states, cities, and counties were authorized to provide jobs for unemployed workers and funds were distributed according to an area's unemployment rate. There were, however, priority persons for assistance under Title VI. These included veterans, disadvantaged workers, and persons who had exceeded their unemployment insurance benefit period. Expenditures for this large program were about .28 per cent of GNP in 1977, but appropriations declined after that.

In 1978 employment under CETA Titles II and VI absorbed 10 per cent of America's jobless or 750,000 workers. In successive years, entitlements declined so that by 1980 only 32,800 persons were employed under CETA.[94] Under the Comprehensive Employment and Training Act job creation activities were authorized under Titles II and VI. Youths were a special target of CETA, but disadvantaged and older workers were also included. CETA IID authorized the Structural Unemployment Program which offered federal funds to states, localities, and counties for hiring unemployed persons in public service jobs within areas where unemployment exceeded 6.5 per cent for three consecutive months. An undesired outcome of this program was that governments substituted federal job funds for other fiscal obligations. Estimates pertaining to the rate at which federal job creation funds were used to support already employed persons and finance existing public jobs range from 20 per cent to 100 per cent. After the 1978 amendments were passed, the CETA IID program placed a much stronger emphasis on jobs for the disadvantaged.

In the early 1980s a public works job creation program was authorized in response to cyclical unemployment, but the principal thrust of job creation activities during this decade has been in the private sector. The Emergency Jobs Act of 1983 was an attempt to respond to the high levels of unemployment caused by the 1981-1982 recession. At the end of a 17-month recessionary period, 10.7 per cent of the work force was unemployed. The Act provided nine billion dollars in federal funds to create temporary jobs in the public sector during a two-year period between 1983 and 1984, including $4.6 billion in direct appropriations. Public works projects included the construction or repair of highways, airports, and other components of the nation's transportation network as well as environmental and prison construction projects. The public works restriction reflected the prevalent national anathema for public service employment which characterized CETA. In that the job creation activities were channeled into construction projects, the program was slow, costly, and tended to benefit white males, many of whom had not been unemployed prior to obtaining a federally sponsored job. Estimates from the U.S. General Accounting Office (GAO) are that 35,000 new jobs were created representing about .6 per cent of the jobs created during the recovery. The impact on unemployment was largely symbolic.

6.4 *The Effects of Income Replacement and Transfer Programs*

Transfer payments to jobless and indigent Americans are the fundamental ingredient of a compensatory labor market policy. Unemployment insurance and other forms of income transfer improve the living standard of jobless Americans, but the impact of these programs has been lessened during the 1980s as a result of legislated budget cutbacks and other economic restraints.

In 1976, the poverty rate among all jobless workers was reduced by 9 per cent as a result of income transfers. Among recipients of unemployment insurance benefits, only 7.5 per cent of workers were below the poverty level after receipt of UI and other social benefits, as compared with 20.7 per cent prior to the transfer. Non-recipients of UI benefits saw less improvement with a decrease of about 7.5 per cent in their poverty rate as a result of income transfers. The difference in the rate of improvement for the two groups in 1976 equaled 6.5 percentage units; in 1983 it was 5.4 percentage points.

In 1983, almost one-third of the jobless would have been in poverty without income transfers. as seen in Table 6.2. After transfers, about one-fourth were below the poverty rate; an improvement of 7.6 per cent. Among recipients of UI benefits, only 13 per cent remained in poverty after income transfers as compared with a rate of 30 per cent among those who were not eligible for UI benefits. For the long-term unemployed, the level of poverty is substantially higher for either group. In 1983, 39 per cent of UI recipients out of work for 51 weeks or more were in poverty and 56 per cent of non UI recipients were below the poverty level after income transfers.[95]

6.5 Evaluations of Labor Market Programs

Employment and training programs have been a focal point of evaluation studies in the United States since the 1960s but despite the attention that has been given to these programs considerable inconsistency exists among studies. In recent years, evaluation studies have demonstrated that methodological factors in previous assessments of employment programs may have led to false conclusions about the relative benefits of program activities upon participants. Researchers have attained a greater appreciation of the intricate relationship between the characteristics of a treatment program and those of the participants and the need to specify differences among programs and beneficiaries as precisely as possible in order to discern the effects of programs upon participants. Previous efforts may have been more beneficial than early evaluations suggested.

TABLE 6.2

Effects of Income Transfers on Poverty Status Among the Unemployed in 1976 and 1983

	All jobless	UI Recipients	Nonrecipients
1976 Poverty rate			
Pre transfer	.240	.207	.255
Post transfer	.154	.075	.188
1983 Poverty rate			
Pre transfer	.323	.244	.362
Post transfer	.247	.132	.304

Source: U. S. Congress, House, Testimony of Wayne Vroman, Urban Institute, Hearing before the Employment and Housing Subcommittee of the Committee on Government Operations, *Changes in The Unemployment Insurance Program: Is the Safety Net Eroding?*, 99th Cong., 2d sess., 22 May 1986.

In addition to reanalyses of programs, reviews of a body of literature have also provided more insight into the effects of labor market programs on placement and earnings. Barnow's review of literature pertaining to studies about earnings gains among CETA participants is a case in point. Looking across a series of evaluation studies, Barnow identifies a pattern of greater earnings increases for female participants than for males and more beneficial effects from public service employment and on-the-job training than from classroom learning experiences. [96]

Indicators of Program Effects. Two indicators of program outcome are the placement rate of program participants and the earnings level of participants. Information regarding program costs, particularly the costs for each person trained or placed is sometimes available.

Studies of the Comprehensive Employment and Training Act (CETA) produce substantially lower estimates of placement than those of the more recent Job Training Partnership Act (JTPA). Seventy per cent of JTPA participants secured employment or entered some other activity after training. Among JTPA program titles, disadvantaged participants experienced an average placement rate of two in three participants, among dislocated workers the rate is slightly higher. Variations in placement levels between CETA and JTPA are indicators of program orientation as much as of program efficiency. Under JTPA, local authorities must set and meet performance standards which cause them to focus on the "employability" of program applicants.

Training costs for each person vary widely by program; as a baseline, placement costs without training for the U.S. Employment Service were $191 for each placement in FY 1985. Among the more cost efficient programs is Title III of JTPA which retrained and relocated dislocated workers at an average cost of $911 per person in 1986 (current dollars). About 69% of the participants in this program found work.

Costs for each participant in the Summer Youth Program funded under Title IIB of JTPA were about $1,000, as shown in Table 6.3. Programs for the disadvantaged, which last about twice as long, had an average individual cost of $1,730 in 1986. The placement rate was 62 per cent. Participant earnings averaged 55 per cent of the national mean.

The Work Incentives Program (WIN), which applies to welfare recipients, has had some success in securing unsubsidized employment for welfare recipients removing some individuals from social dependency. National data on employment and independency are reported in Table 6.4. The number of persons securing jobs has declined, but not as rapidly as the level of appropriations. Cost savings information available for 1981 and 1982 indicate savings in welfare payments of $160 and $521 million yearly attributable to employment. Data from the State of Massachusetts show a net savings of $1,076 million in AFDC payments for calendar year 1986. In another study of five programs, reductions of 11 per cent, 8 per cent, 4 per cent, 1 per cent, and zero in average welfare payments were observed.[97]

Work and Welfare Programs. During the 1980s welfare employment programs have become an increasingly significant component of American social policy. The states execute special employment programs for recipients of Aid For Families with Dependent Children (AFDC) benefits. Evidence compiled by the U.S. GAO from four state demonstration programs found that about one-third of welfare recipients were placed in jobs with

TABLE 6.3

Management Indicators for the Job Training Partnership Act, FY 1986

	Title IIA Disadvantage	Title III Dislocated	Title IIB Summer Youth
Participants	1,097,057	211,057	616,945
Terminees %	55%	66%	5%
	1,096,057	211,057	
Entered Work Force %	62%	69%	N/A
Cost per participant	$1,730	$911	$1,000
Average wage	4.72	6.61	N/A
Per cent of U. S. Average (National $8.52)	55%	78%	N/A
Average weeks of training	18	20	N/A

(N/A = not available)
Source: Unpublished data, U.S. Department of Labor; U.S. General Accounting Office, Dislocated Workers, March 1987.

average earnings above the minimum wage. The majority of jobs were full time but more than one-fourth in each state were part-time jobs.

Placement costs in the state programs varied widely from over $3,000 for each person in Massachusetts, a state which offers extensive support services to working mothers, to $457 in Texas. A large share of AFDC recipients were removed from welfare under these programs. In Massachusetts, 86 per cent of the AFDC grants were closed for more than 360 days which partly offsets its large placement cost. In Michigan, AFDC benefits were ended for 61 per cent of participants and in Texas 56 per cent were taken off the welfare roster at a cost of $457 for each participant. The data reported in Table 6.5 reveal inconsistencies in state recordkeeping.

Welfare recipients typically exit and re-enter dependency, but studies using experimental and control groups have produced similar findings. Among treated group members in the City of San Diego, employment was six percentage points higher and earnings were 23 percentage points greater than among control group members who did not participate in the work program. The San Diego experiment indicates that job search combined with job training assistance provided the most consistent post-program

TABLE 6.4

WIN Program Statistics, FY 1981-1986

	1981	1982	1984	1985	1986
Persons entering unsubsidized employment (1000s)	310	204	354	340	260
Persons completely off welfare due to employment (1000s)	169	144	178	170	130
Welfare Cost Savings (millions)	760	521	N/A	N/A	N/A

Source: U.S. Congress, House, Committee on Ways and Means, Background Material and Data on Programs Within the Jurisdiction of the Committee, 100th Cong., 1st sess., 6 March 1987.

TABLE 6.5

WIN Program Statistics from Four States, 1986

	Massachusetts	Michigan	Texas	Oregon
Placements (N)	12,870	——	19,509	18,324
Placement rate (%)	38	——	37	——
Full-time share (%)	68	——	71	65
Average Wage (Hourly)	$5.45			$4.09
subgroup of placements		$4.70	$3.76	
AFDC Grant closure of				
360 days (%)	86	61	56	——
Placement cost	$3,333	——	$457	$658

Source: U.S. General Accounting Office, Work and Welfare: Analysis of AFDC Employment Programs in Four States, January 1988.

employment and the greatest improvements in earnings.[98] Findings from the study are presented in Table 6.6.

Previous researchers have observed that the impact of employment and training programs varies among different demographic groups. Women's earnings tend to show greater increases after training than men's ranging between $1500 and $999 more yearly. Less positive gains have been found for men and young people. On-the-job experience provided a greater impact on earnings than classroom experience or public service employment with average gains of $850 each year. On-the-job training translated

TABLE 6.6

Employment and Earnings Impact of Five Work-Welfare Programs
with Experimental and Control Group Evaluations

	Difference in Employment %	Difference in Average Earnings %
City of San Diego	+10	+23
City of Baltimore	+16	+10
State of Arkansas	+34	+37
State of Virginia	+8	+8
State of W. Virginia	-2	0

Source: Judith M. Gueron, *Work-Welfare Programs*, New Directions for Program
Evaluation, no. 37, 1988. Data derived from official final reports.

into $1200 more annually for minority females, whereas white males gained
about $550 each year.[99]
    The Job Corps, which targets disadvantaged young people, is one of the
oldest employment programs in the United States. It was originally
established in 1964. The main thrust of the program is to train young
persons for work by providing basic education and on-the-job training.
Youths are housed in separate work sites away from their family. Some
centers are administered by contracted agents and others are administered
as Civilian Conservation Centers (CCC). Evidence suggests that the type of
administration is related to different program outcomes. Of these outcomes, placement rates and earnings levels are of interest here. Because of
the high per capita costs of the Job Corps program it has been under scrutiny
for many years.
    Costs for training Job Corps participants vary widely with the nature of
the program. Of the CCC programs, the average annual cost was $14,776 in
1984. Contract centers were cheaper to operate with an average individual
cost of $10,545. Although part of the difference is attributed to housing costs
($1,157), a GAO study found that the government-run centers offered
substantially more training in trades and crafts skills; the contract centers
focus on training for service occupations including clerical and health care
fields.[100]

These differences are reflected in the initial earnings levels of program participants. Persons trained in government-run centers earned $4.47 hourly in comparison with an average of $3.91 for trainees from centers operated by contractors, as shown in Table 6.7.

TABLE 6.7

Job Corps Program Information, 1984

Center Type	Positive Exit %	Cost per Person	Average Wage per Hour
Government-Run	84.2	$14,776	$4.47
Contractor-Run	70.9	$10,545	$3.91

Source: U.S. General Accounting Office, Job Corps: Its Costs, Employment Outcomes and Service to the Public, July 1986.

Persons who did not remain in the CCC program at least 90 days earned $3.80 hourly, while those from contract centers earned only $3.69 per hour. These data suggest that for the sample of youths involved in Job Corps programs initial earnings gains are associated with participation levels.

Completion of the program or survival for at least 90 days are also determinants of successful placement upon exit. More than 90 per cent of those who met these criteria found jobs upon leaving the CCC. For youth in contract centers, 70 per cent of those with 90 days experience and 78 per cent of those completing this program were successfully placed.

Similar to the Job Corps, the Supported Works program which operated between 1975 and 1981 targeted especially hard to employ youths. A recent evaluation of the long term effects of the program in five urban areas indicates that the nature of the work experience is a critical determinant of program success. For hard to employ urban youths highly structured supported work environments appear to have had greater positive results than mainstream public service employment experiences. [101]

Job Creation Programs. Job creation programs in the public sector have not been popular during the 1980s and public service employment was excluded from the Job Training Partnership Act, the principal employment legislation of the period. Earlier in the decade, the U.S. used public funds to create jobs in response to high rates of unemployment created by the recession of 1981-1982.

Historically, the U.S. has not been quick to respond to cyclical swings in the economy. In addition to the problem of recognizing the start of an economic downturn, the U.S. Congress must formulate and enact legislation to ameliorate the problem that is acceptable to bipartisan committee members and can be approved by the Congress and President. Finally, if authorized, funds must be transmitted to the agencies or jurisdictions authorized to execute the program. Typically, more than two years elapse from the start of an economic recession and the enactment of a federal response. In the last recession (1981-1982), the Emergency Jobs Act of 1983 was passed 21 months after the recession began. Considerable political posturing occurs in the process of determining whether and how the Congress should respond to economic conditions.[102]

The legislation developed to address the problem of high unemployment avoided the politically unpalatable idea of public service employment by authorizing expenditures for temporary public works projects. But public works projects, which were politically preferable to public service jobs, were much slower to implement and the speed with which recovery funds could be pumped into the economy was hampered by this condition.[103] The Congress understood the necessity of expediting expenditures in order to maximize the impact of public funds on the rate of recovery and included provisions for expenditure rates in the legislation that was enacted March 24, 1983. The Act set June 1984 as a target date for the expenditure of the nine billion dollars authorized. Studies by the U.S. General Accounting Office (GAO), however, determined that one year after the target date half of the authorized funds remained unused. Table 6.8 reports information on spending rates for programs in the GAO study.

TABLE 6.8

Spending Rate of Funds Under the Emergency Jobs Act of 1983

		Funds in Millions	
Funds spent by:	September 1983	June 1984	June 1985
Available Funds	$9,029	$9,029	$9,029
Funds Spent	$1,319	$3,062	$4,487
Per cent of available funds	15%	34%	50%

Source: U.S. General Accounting Office, Emergency Jobs Act of 1983 Funds Spent Slowly, Few Jobs Created, December 1986, 28.

The estimated impact of the nine billion dollars authorized for expenditure under the Emergency Jobs Act after substitution effects was a reduction in the rate of unemployment of .6 per cent[104]—a rather poor but typical performance.[105] Moreover, the beneficiaries of the program were predominantly white males. Less than 15 per cent of those receiving jobs in public works projects were female, which is not surprising since the majority of jobs created were in the construction industry. Less than one-third of the beneficiaries were members of racial or ethnic minorities. Finally, about 35 per cent of those who were employed under the Emergency Jobs Act were not previously unemployed.

In exploring the extent to which local official attempted to provide employment opportunities for the unemployed with the funds available for public works projects, a classic example of the effects of implementation on program outcomes was identified. While a number of projects made full effort to assure that the maximum number of jobless secured work with the funds allocated, others made little effort to hire unemployed persons, considering them inappropriate candidates for the tasks to be filled. In one case, a local government in Massachusetts asserted that the public works project they executed under the Emergency Jobs Act required persons highly skilled in construction crafts who would not be found among the unemployed. Consequently, they contracted the work to a private sector firm from Louisiana which used its own crew to execute the complete job. As a result the employment opportunities went to employed persons who resided outside the targeted area. [106]

6.6 Social Impacts

Studies that evaluate the effects of labor market programs upon program participants are one indicator of program impact. But the overall effects of public policies on society also provide meaningful indicators of social performance. Information about broad social indicators are useful for that purpose.

Economic Equality. In a study of equality in the United States, Gary Burtless, a Brookings Institute fellow, found strong evidence of increased economic inequality among Americans in the current decade. Running counter to the popular belief that a rising tide raises all boats, in recent years economic growth has led to greater distances between the poorest and richest members of American society.[107] A number of other studies identify increasing levels of income inequality in the United States and longitudinal analyses suggest that gains in economic equality underway during the 1960s have been lost in the last two decades.[108]

The distribution of all family income reflects this shift. While there has been little change within the share of income going to the middle class, poor families received a smaller portion of national family income in 1984 than they did in 1969, and the wealthiest families received a larger share of national family income during the same period. Among families in poverty, the proportion headed by females has more than doubled between 1949 and 1984.[109]

The proportion of families in the U.S. living below the federal poverty index declined steadily from 18.1 per cent in 1960 to 9.7 per cent in 1969, at which time the living standard of five million families was below the poverty level. The lowest proportion of families in poverty occurred in 1974 and 1975 at 8.8 per cent or slightly less than five million families. In 1982 and 1983, more than 12 per cent of all families existed below the poverty level. The number of poor families exceeded 7 million through 1985.

As the data in Table 6.9 indicate, non-white families and those headed by a female are much more likely to exist below the poverty level. Among

TABLE 6.9

Families in Poverty by Race and Female Head of Household, 1970-1985

Year	Families Below Poverty %	Non- White %	With Female Head of Household %
1970	10.1	29.5	32.5
1971	10.0	28.8	33.9
1972	9.3	29.0	32.7
1973	8.8	28.1	32.2
1974	8.8	26.9	32.1
1975	9.7	27.1	32.5
1976	9.4	27.9	33.0
1977	9.3	28.2	31.7
1978	9.1	27.5	31.4
1979	9.2	27.8	30.4
1980	10.3	28.9	32.7
1981	11.2	30.8	34.6
1982	12.2	33.0	36.3
1983	12.3	32.3	36.0
1984	11.6	30.9	34.5
1985	11.4	28.7	34.0

Source: U.S. Council of Economic Advisors, Economic Report of the President, Washington: D.C.: GPO, 1987, Table B-29.

non-white families, the rate of poverty jumped after 1980, exceeding 30 per cent of all families, but since 1985 the proportion of poor families has declined slightly. In cases where women are the head of household, the proportion in poverty exceeds 30 per cent. This is actually an improvement over the rates in the early 1960s, but the number of families headed by women has increased substantially over time. In 1985, 3.5 million female householders were in poverty status, while the number in 1960 was 2.0 million. Poverty levels among non-white women who are household heads are very high; the proportion has drifted around 50 per cent since 1960. About one-fourth of white female heads of household live in poverty. As is the case with white women, there is no clear pattern of improvement in the poverty rate over time.[110]

In attempting to explain the causes of growing inequality, researchers have considered a number of factors. The effects of wage differentials and growing levels of unemployment are identified by Burtless as contributing factors along with the ineffectiveness of American social policy. Burtless argues that redistributive policies are needed to produce a short-term improvement in income disparity, but he raises important concerns about the willingness of the American public to support such a policy. [111]

A focal point in these discussions has been the declining wage rate in the United States and the proportion of newly created jobs that offer relatively low pay. Harrison and Bluestone present findings showing that the 48 per cent of the jobs created between 1979 and 1985 paid wages below the median whereas in the period between 1973 and 1979 only one-third of the jobs fell below the median wage which, along with other indicators, lead them to conclude that America has made a "U turn" on the road to economic equality. In assessing the effects of service industry growth in metropolitan areas, other researchers have concluded that low wage jobs in this industry partly account for the disadvantageous economic status among certain groups of people—particularly youths, minorities, and women.[112]

Risk of Unemployment. Evidence of increased economic disparity is one reason for concern about the U.S. labor market. A second factor is related to apparent increases in the jeopardy that working Americans face with respect to job loss and the the more severe consequences of unemployment that exist in the 1980s. While the rate of employment in 1988 is growing and the level of unemployment steadily declining, certain aspects of the labor market are disconcerting. More workers in part-time and temporary status translates into more people without job security and employment related benefits such as health insurance and pensions. The rate of insured unemployment has declined sharply from 50 per cent in 1974 to 33 per cent in 1986. At the same time, the duration of unemployment has been higher during the 1980s than in preceding decades. Finally, the proportion of persons exhausting their benefit coverage has drifted upward since the mid-1970s. Jeopardy to the worker is increased by greater consequences of unemployment.

If the current balance between the supply and demand for labor is fragile, as the reliance upon contingent workers suggests it might be, there appears to be a risk that workers in non-permanent positions will be shed as the demand for labor diminishes. Thus greater jeopardy also exists for these temporary and part-time workers whose connection to the work force is based upon continued economic recovery. Workers at the periphery of the labor force are at the greatest risk and it can be argued that they insulate core workers from the effects of economic swings by their weak bonds to the market. Jeopardy to the worker is thus increased by a labor market that offers little employment security.

It has been argued that U.S. economic policy is directed toward the core of society and makes symbolic responses to the needs of those on the fringe of the social fabric. To the extent that this is true, workers at risk should not expect to be rescued by public policies that might not be forthcoming.

6.7 The Policy Making Process and Implementation Factors

The policy making process in place in the United States is distinctively different from those found in other Western nations and the administrative machinery for implementing national policy directives is much more diverse. It can be argued that in the area of employment policy, the nature of the process does not enhance the realization of policy goals.

Consensus is the key ingredient of policy formation in the Congress. Initiative thus awaits a consensus that action is required and policy outputs are the product of bargaining and cooperation. In the area of employment policy where a national agreement on government's role and the responsibility of individual workers is absent, consensus building delays response. Yet employment problems typically require immediate, if not anticipatory, action. Because of these delays, consensus building minimizes the impact of employment policy outputs and in the case of countercyclical measures, delays may completely nullify the effects of program efforts.

Ginsburg's study of efforts to pass the Humphrey-Hawkins Full Employment Act in the U.S. Congress depict the consensus building struggle as well as its effects on employment policy outputs. The legislation, which was first introduced in 1974 and finally passed in 1978, lacked any real commitment to achieve the goal of full employment and has essentially been ignored. Ginsburg concluded, "The struggle for Humphrey-Hawkins, its watering down, and its subsequent neglect thus mirror in part the weakness of the movement for full employment."[113] The experience is typical of American employment policy development.

In attempting to respond to labor market problems, the Congress tends to overlook their generic nature. Instead each event is treated as a unique one. Consequently, little is done to integrate related programs or identify connections across time periods and program areas. Policy outputs are often too narrow in scope to be effective.

Although the methodology for evaluating program impacts has become increasingly sophisticated, knowledge about the intricate relationships between program characteristics and individual success has not been translated into operation. The complexity of the information and the bureaucratic inclination to develop generalized programs and practices work against the attainment of programs that meet the special needs of different participants.

At the same time, the structure of the American federal system and the diversity of actors and agencies continuously involved in public policy implementation enhances the potential for program delays and interorganizational conflicts. To the extent that public policies are characterized by multiple objectives and competing goals, conflicts are likely to occur between program areas as well as among the different levels of government.

The absence of centralized administration of programs is clearly felt not only in the lack of coordination among the bureaucratic actors, but also in the time required for public agencies to "gear-up" to respond to congressional mandates for action.

Moreover, the decentralized structure of employment policy implementation impedes the agenda setting process. While the different bureaucratic participants may be keenly aware of pending and future areas of employment policy requiring action, decentralization does not produce a voice of sufficient strength to secure the attention of policy makers. Special interests cannot be balanced by a weak bureaucracy, and the labor market agenda is driven by the need to obtain a consensus among these competing interests. As Heidenheimer, Heclo, and Adams observed:

> ...the United States has created what appears, in a comparative perspective, to be a well-functioning mechanism for building policy consensus. But precisely because so much effort is invested in building the consensus, the mechanism exhibits very little capacity for moving that consensus.[114]

Policy making processes and the machinery for implementing policy objectives ironically often servce as barriers to achieving policy goals.

6.8 Policy Outcomes

The question of the extent to which government outputs are responsive to labor market factors has been pursued by other researchers. One such effort, executed by Thomas Janoski, compared the determinants of active labor market policy expenditures in the United States and West Germany and found that the principal determinants of policy outcomes differ in the two countries. While spending on labor market measures in West Germany is responsive to levels of unemployment, in the case of the United States, government appears to be unresponsive to increasing levels of jobless-ness.[115]

Instead, the strongest factors accounting for labor market policy expenditures are related to the supply of labor, including population growth on the one hand and labor force participation on the other. Another important factor is the effect of external pressures on the market, most clearly indicated by the reaction to the oil shortage crisis. The effects of the political process were measured by the distribution of political party representatives on key congressional committees and the presence of the Reagan Administration. The effects of bureaucratic factors, the policymaking process, or govern-mental sluggishness (which accounts for considerable lag time between economic events and political outcomes) did not prove statistically signifi-cant in the final analysis. Janoski's "socialization model" explained more than 90 per cent of the variance in labor market policy expenditures in the U.S.[116]

The results of his study and the striking differences between the American and West German models, emphasize the lack of integration between American labor market policy and economic policy. As Janoski concludes, "An internal system of political economy does not operate consistently...."[117] Policy output may occur as a result of political demands derived from an oversupply of labor. As crowding in the market increases, the demands for a political response intensify, and a policy output in the form of increased allocations is eventually produced. Another catalyst for action, Janoski observed, is pressure from outside the market in that the political parties are more likely to arrive at a political compromise that produces a successful piece of legislation in response to an external threat.

Enacted legislation and appropriations are only indicators of outputs in that as observed earlier, expenditures patterns often do not maximize available funds and sluggishness in the distribution of resources dilutes their impact. Thus the actual response may be less than the announced action. But to a large extent, the public may be placated by the appearance of action and demands for further responsiveness. In that power centers are fragmented and uncoordinated and in that the policy outputs are directed toward those at the periphery of the system, there is no voice to demand political accountability.

It is not surprising that policy outputs are largely symbolic and compensatory in nature; nor is it inconsistent that beneficiaries of policy outputs are typically identified by need standards. It is not merely the absence of an integrated labor market policy or of an administrative apparatus to execute and coordinate policy directives that accounts for the lack of responsiveness in the American system, but rather that the policy process fails to respond to internal cues about the need for adjustments in labor market policy. Thus, use of the term "active labor market policy" seems inappropriate in the U.S. case.

6.9 Summary

Descriptive information has been put forward as a basis against which to judge the performance of U.S. labor market policy over the last two decades. It was argued earlier that the United States lacks an active labor market policy pursuing instead a compensatory approach designed to ameliorate the condition of people at the periphery of society. There is evidence that the social goals of the preceding years have been partly achieved, particularly with respect to discrimination in employment and compensation of women and minorities. But in taking a broad view of the development of employment policies, evidence of some retreat from the social concerns of the 1960s is apparent. Today's policies have a distinct employer-orientation and the scope and investment in employment, training and job creation programs has clearly declined during the 1980s. In the United States, in the absence of employment policies, the effects of market forces are also powerful determinants of winners and losers in a national economy. Unanticipated structural changes, changes in technology, and cyclical economic periods have also left their mark.

Of the diverse segments of the U.S. population, some persons have clearly benefited from employment policies. Women, whose rate of unemployment is now equivalent to men's, are one group of winners. But at the same time, women who were displaced from their jobs and stopped trying to find new work are clear losers. Women have increased their rate of labor force participation, and some who have penetrated formerly male occupations have benefited from better wages and greater job security. On the other hand, women who have pursued careers in low-paying service sector jobs, in the part-time, and temporary work force are all losers in that their rate of pay, job security and benefits generally lag behind the market.

Black women, in particular, have shown clear gains in their earnings relative to white women's pay, but the picture for blacks overall is not as strong. Among the greatest losers under current policies are minority youths, who suffer extraordinarily high levels of unemployment and who lack adequate skills for job placement.

Workers displaced from stable employment in manufacturing have lost wages as well as career progression. While many have recuperated, others have found lower paying jobs and some have become discouraged from trying to find work. Low-skilled and minimally educated workers have fewer opportunities.

Hispanic workers appear to have fared better. Their rate of labor force participation has climbed, including less traditional work outside the house for Hispanic women. Their rate of unemployment is much lower than the rate for blacks and their educational achievements are less limiting with respect to labor force participation.

Workers-across-the-board have experienced a decline in the real value of their wages and the distribution of income has become more skewed, increasing the distance between the rich and poor segments of society.

Workers in the emerging industry of contingent workers and members of the expanding part-time work force appear to be at risk of unemployment in an economy that may have reached a fragile balance between labor supply and demand.

For those who do become unemployed, the likelihood of receiving unemployment insurance benefits has greatly declined and the rate of earnings replacement is also lower. There appears to be an increase in the duration of unemployment. Thus workers are at greater jeopardy from the consequences of unemployment.

In summary, those who are peripheral workers with respect to their skills and status as employees or who work in peripheral industries have seen their risk of unemployment increase and their benefits from employment decline. It is important not to lose sight of the fact that many workers have benefited from policies pursued in the United States, particularly those concerning equal employment opportunity and career advancement. Policies in the United States have focused on special groups of workers and have often limited their effort to members of special population groups.

As such the country lacks a cohesive employment policy and has little ability to respond to structural or cyclical swings in the pattern of joblessness. At the beginning of the 1980s, a deep recession created high levels of unemployment and much suffering. The response of the U.S. Congress, the Emergency Jobs Act of 1983, was a potentially useful remedy but the prescription arrived too late and the medicine was administered too slowly to have any real impact on the recovery. If recession comes again to the U.S. this decade, there is little indication that the country will be more prepared or that the pattern of suffering will be different.

Notes

Chapter 1

1. F. Ray Marshall, Allan G. King, and Vernon M. Briggs, Jr., *Labor Economics* (Homewood, Illinois: Irwin, 1980), 537-542.

2. Robert Y. Shapiro, et al., "The Polls—A Report: Employment and Social Welfare," *Public Opinion Quarterly* 51 (Summer 1987):275.

Chapter 2

3. *The Washington Post*, National Weekly Edition, 9 February 1987, derived from *Washington Post*-ABC News Polls.

4. F. Ray Marshall, Allan G. King, and Vernon M. Briggs, Jr., *Labor Economics* (Homewood, Illinois: Irwin, 1980), 537-542.

5. Marshall, et al., *Labor Economics*, 1980, 537-542.

6. U.S., Congress, House, Testimony of John G. Bickerman of the Center on Budget and Policy Priorities before the Subcommittee on Employment and Housing of the Committee on Government Operations, *Changes in the Unemployment Insurance Program: Is the Safety Net Eroding?*, 99th Cong., 2d sess., 22 May 1986, 13-18.

7. U.S., Bureau of Labor Statistics (BLS), *Labor Force Statistics Derived from the Consumer Population Survey: A Databook*, vol. 1 (Washington, DC: Government Printing Office (GPO), September 1982, Table B26.

8. BLS, "Job Search of Recipients of Unemployment Insurance," *Monthly Labor Review* 102 (February 1979):52.

9. Thomas Janoski, "The Political Economy of Unemployment: Active Labor Market Policy in West Germany and the United States," Doctoral Dissertation, Duke University, 1986, 168-171.

10. Betsy Taylor and Robert W. Bednarzik, "U. S. Treatment of Displaced Workers," unpublished paper, August 1986.

11. Philip L. Martin, *Labor Displacement and Public Policy* (Lexington, MA: Lexington Books, 1983), 110-117.

12. U.S., Congress, House, Committee on Ways and Means, *Background Material and Data on Programs within the Jurisdiction of the Committee on Ways and Means*, 100th Cong., 1st sess., 6 March 1987.

13. U.S., Congress, *Congressional Quarterly Weekly Report* 46 (2 January 1988).

14. Gunther Schmid, *Labour Market Policy in Transition* (Stockholm: EFA, 1988); Jan Johannesson, "On the Composition and Outcome of Swedish Labor Market Policy: 1970-1987," Stockholm: EFA, 1987.

15. Janoski, "The Political Economy of Unemployment," 1986, 168-171.

Chapter 3
16. U.S., Bureau of Labor Statistics (BLS), "Projections 2000: The Changing Labor Force," *Occupational Outlook Quarterly* 31 (Fall 1987):12.
17. BLS, *Employment in Perspective: Minority Workers*, nos. 730 and 744, 1987.
18. Organization for Cooperation and Development (OECD), *Employment Outlook* (September 1987):60.
19. BLS, *Employment in Perspective: Women in the Labor Force, 1986*, no. 730, 1986; BLS, "Children of Working Mothers," Bulletin no. 2158, March 1983; BLS, *News*, 87-345, August 1987.
20. OECD, *Employment Outlook* (September 1987):197; BLS, *Employment and Earnings* 35 (January 1988):Table 1.
21. U.S., Bureau of the Census, *Statistical Abstract of the U.S.*, 107th ed. (Washington, DC: GPO, 1987), Table 198; BLS, *Employment and Earnings 35 (January 1988)*:Table 3.
22. Wayne J. Howe, "Education and Demographics: How Do They Affect Unemployment Rates?" *Monthly Labor Review* 111 (January 1988):7; U.S., Bureau of the Census, *Statistical Abstract of the United States*, 107th ed. (Washington, DC: Government Printing Office (GPO), 1987), Table 198; BLS, *News*, 85-355, October 1985, and 97-415, September 1987.
23. BLS, *Employment and Earnings* 35 (January 1988):Table 6.
24. Robert W. Bednarzik, "Involuntary Part-time Work: A Cyclical Analysis," *Monthly Labor Review* 98 (September 1975):13.
25. BLS, *Monthly Labor Review* 111 (February 1988):Table 6.
26. William Serrin, "Part-time Work, New Labor Trend," *New York Times*, 9 July 1986; "Fragile Economy Seen in Temporary Job Rise," *New York Times*, 16 March 1988.
27. Wayne J. Howe, "Temporary Help Workers: Who They Are, What Jobs They Hold," *Monthly Labor Review* 109 (November 1986):46.
28. U. S., General Accounting Office (GAO), Briefing Report to the Chairman, Committee on Post Office and Civil Service, House of Representatives, *Federal Workforce: New Authority to Make and Extend Temporary Appointments* (Washington, DC: GAO, July 1986), 13.
29. GAO, Fact Sheet for the Chairman, Subcommittee on Civil Service, Post Office and General Services, Committee on Governmental Affairs, U.S. Senate, *Federal Workforce: Views on Need to Offer Health Insurance to Temporary Employees* (Washington, DC: GAO, June 1987).
30. Wayne J. Howe, "Temporary Help Workers," November 1986, 46.
31. Valerie A. Personick, "Industry Output and Employment through the End of the Century," *Monthly Labor Review* 110 (September 1987) 31-32.
32. BLS, *Employment and Earnings* 34 (June 1987):Table C-2.
33. Robert W. Bednarzik, "An Examination of the Shift in Jobs from the Goods to the Service Sector in the U.S.," Paper presented at OECD meeting, Tokyo, 15-19 June 1987, 23.
34. Bednarzik, "Examination of the Shift in Jobs," 1987, 26.

35. Bednarzik, "Examination of the Shift in Jobs," 1987, 19-23.

36. U.S., Bureau of the Census, *Statistical Abstract*, 1987, Table 467.

37. U.S., Bureau of Economic Analysis, *Survey of Current Business*, 63 (July 1983) through 67(July 1987).

38. Bureau of Economic Analysis, *Survey of Current Business*, 1983-1987.

39. B. Guy Peters, "The United States: Absolute Change and Relative Stability," in *Public Employment in Western Nations* ed. R. Rose (Cambridge: Cambridge University Press, 1985), 228-261.

40. Bureau of the Census, *Statistical Abstract*, 1987, computed from Table 468.

Chapter 4

41. Katherine G. Abraham, "Help-Wanted Advertising, Job Vacancies, and Unemployment," *Brookings Papers on Economic Activity*, 1987, 1:228.

42. Harvey A. Garn, *Labor Market Analysis and Public Policy* (Washington, DC: Urban Institute, 1970).

43. Abraham, "Help Wanted Advertising," 1987, 225.

44. Abraham, "Help Wanted Advertising," 1987, 225.

45. Bennett Harrision and Barry Bluestone, "The Dark Side of Labour Market 'Flexibility': Falling Wages and Growing Income Inequality in America," Labour Market Analysis and Employment Planning, working paper no. 17 (Geneva: International Labour Organization (ILO), 1987): 30-35.

46. Lois Recascino Wise, "Dimensions of Public Sector Pay Administration," *Review of Public Personnel Administration* 8 (Summer 1988):66-70.

47. Richard S. Belous, "Flexibility and American Labour Markets: The Evidence and Implications," Labour Market Analysis and Employment Planning, working paper no. 14 (Geneva: ILO, June 1987), 16-19.

48. Richard Cantor and John Wenninger, "Current Labor Market Trends and Inflation," *Federal Reserve Bank of New York Quarterly Review* 12 (Autumn 1987):36-48; Robert G. Sheets, Stephen Nord and John J. Phelps, *The Impact of Service Industries on Underemployment in Metropolitan Economies* (Lexington, MA: Lexington Books, 1987), 55-62.

49. U.S., Council of Economic Advisors, *Economic Report of the President* (Washington, DC: Government Printing Office (GPO), January 1987), 220-225.

50. Harrison and Bluestone, "The Dark Side of Labour Market 'Flexibility,'" 1987, 40-43.

51. U.S., Bureau of Labor Statistics (BLS), *Employment in Perspective: Women in the Labor Force*, no. 739, 1987.

52. Organization for Economic Cooperation and Development (OECD), *Employment Outlook*, (September 1986):19; OECD, *Flexibility in the Labour Market: The Current Debate* (Paris: OECD, 1986):51.

53. Ellen Sehgal, "Occupational Mobility and Job Tenure in 1983," *Monthly Labor Review* 107 (October 1984):22.

54. Sehgal, "Occupational Mobility," October 1984, 20-22.

55. Sehgal, "Occupational Mobility," October 1984, 20.

56. Nancy F. Rytina, "Occupational Changes and Tenure, 1981," *Tenure and Occupational Change, 1981*, BLS Bulletin no. 2162 (Washington, DC: GPO, January 1983), 4-8.

57. Sehgal, "Occupational Mobility," October 1984, 21.

58. BLS, *News*, 87-452, October 1987.

59. Larry Long, *Migration and Residential Mobility in the United States*, New York: Russell Sage Foundation, 1988.

60. Calvin L. Beale and Glenn V. Fuguitt, "Metropolitan and Nonmetropolitan Growth Differentials in the United States Since 1980," Center for Demography and Ecology, working paper 85-6, (Madison, WI: CDE, 1985).

61. Beale and Fuguitt, "Metropolitan and Nonmetropolitan Growth Differentials," 1985.

62. *New York Times*, 25 December 1987.

63. Issues of U.S. Bureau of the Census, *Geographical Mobility*, Current Population Reports, Population Characteristics, Series P-20, 1960-70-80.

64. Bureau of the Census, *Geographical Mobility*, Series P-20, no. 407, September 1986, 4.

65. Long, *Migration and Residential Mobility*, 1988.

66. James G. March and Herbert A. Simon, *Organizations* (New York: John Wiley, 1958), 83-111.

Chapter 5

67. U.S., Bureau of Labor Statistics (BLS), *Monthly Labor Review* 100 (September 1987):94, 119.

68. Arthur M. Okun, "Potential GNP: Its Measurements and Significance," in *Economic Policymaking* ed. Joseph Pechman (Cambridge, MA: Massachusetts Institute of Technology, 1983), 145-158.

69. Organization for Economic Cooperation and Development (OECD), *Employment Outlook* (September 1987):177.

70. BLS, *Employment in Perspective: Women in the Labor Force*, No. 731, 1986.

71. BLS, *Employment in Perspective: Women in the Labor Force*, No. 743, 1987.

72. OECD, *Employment Outlook* (September 1986):106-133.

73. Jerome Culp and Bruce Dunson, "Brothers of a Different Color," in *The Black Youth Employment Crisis* ed. R. Freeman and H.J. Holzer (Chicago: The University of Chicago Press, 1986), 233-259; BLS, *Employment in Perspective: Minority Workers*, No. 699, May 1983; No. 746, September 1987.

74. Francine Blau and Marianne Ferber, *The Economics of Women, Men and Work* (Englewood Cliffs, N.J.: Prentice Hall, 1986), 293.

75. Larry DeBoer and Michael Seeborg, "The Female-Male Unemployment Differential: Effects of Change in Industry Employment," *Monthly Labor Review* 107 (November 1984):9-10; M. Seeborg and L. DeBoer, "The Narrowing Male-Female Unemployment Differential," *Growth and Change*, 12(Spring 1987):24-37.

76. Mathematica Policy Research, Inc., *Digest of Data on Persons with Disabilities* (Washington, DC: Congressional Research Service, 1984), Table V.1.

77. U.S., Bureau of the Census, *Statistical Abstract of the United States*, 98th ed. (Washington, DC: Government Printing Office (GPO), 1978), Table 544.

78. Louis Harris & Associates, Inc., *The ICD Survey of Disabled Americans: Bringing Disabled Americans into the Mainstream*, Study no. 854009 (New York: International Center for the Disabled and National Council on the Handicapped,

1986); Robert Haveman, V. Halberstadt, & R.V. Burkhauser, *Public Policy Toward Disabled Workers* (New York: Cornell University Press, 1984), 16-25.

79. BLS, *News*, 86-125, March 1986.

80. Bureau of the Census, *Statistical Abstract*, 1975: Table 571.

81. Francis W. Horvarth, "The Pulse of Economic Change: Displaced Workers of 1981-1985," *Monthly Labor Review* 107 (June 1987):7.

82. Horvarth, "The Pulse of Economic Change," June 1987, 5.

83. Horvarth, "The Pulse of Economic Change," June 1987, 9.

84. H. Peter Gray, Thomas Pugel and Ingo Walter, *International Trade, Employment and Structural Adjustment: The United States* (Geneva: International Labour Organization (ILO), 1986), 61.

85. OECD, *Employment Outlook* (September 1987):142-170.

86. OECD, *Employment Outlook* (September 1987):144.

87. U.S., Congress, House, Committee on Ways and Means, *Background Material and Data on Programs within the Jurisdiction of the Committee on Ways and Means*, 100th Cong., 1st sess., 6 March 1987, 383.

88. BLS, "Linking Employment Problems to Economic Status," Bulletin no. 2282 (Washington, DC: GPO, August 1987), Table 17.

89. U.S., Congress, House, Testimony of John G. Bickerman of the Center for Budget and Policy Priorities before the Subcommittee on Employment and Housing of the Committee on Government Operations, *Changes in the Unemployment Insurance System: Is the Safety Net Eroding?*, 99th Cong., 2d sess., 22 May 1986, 19.

90. Commissioner Janet Norwood quoted in *New York Times*, 20 October 1986.

Chapter 6

91. Jonathan Grossman, *The Department of Labor* (New York: Praeger, 1973), 121.

92. U.S., Congress, Senate, *Congressional Record*, 99th Cong., 2d sess., 1986, 132: S7694-7695.

93. Richard P. Nathan, R.F. Cook, and V.L. Rawlins, *Public Service Employment* (Washington, D.C.: Brookings, 1981), 2-5.

94. Nathan et al., *Public Service Employment*, 1981, 5.

95. U.S., Congress, House, Testimony of Wayne Vroman of the Urban Institute before the Subcommittee on Employment and Housing of the Committee on Government Operations, *Changes in the Unemployment Insurance Program: Is the Safety Net Eroding?*, 99th Cong., 2d sess., 22 May 1986, 43.

96. Burt S. Barnow, "The Impact of CETA Programs on Earnings," *Journal of Human Resources* 22 (Winter 1987):157-159.

97. U.S., Congress, Senate, Committee on Labor and Human Resources, *Work and Welfare*, 100th Cong., 1st sess., 21 January and 3 and 4 February 1987, 93; Judith M. Gueron, *Work-Welfare Programs*, New Directions for Program Evaluation, no. 37 (San Francisco: Jossey-Bass, 1988).

98. Gueron, *Work-Welfare Programs*, 1988.

99. Barnow, "The Impact of CETA Programs," 1987, 168.

100. U.S., General Accounting Office (GAO), Briefing Report to the Chairman, Committee on Labor and Human Resources, U.S. Senate, *Job Corps: Its Costs, Employment Outcomes and Service to the Public* (Washington, DC: GAO, July 1986), 8.

101. David A. Long, "Analyzing Social Program Production: An Assessment of Supported Work for Youths," *Journal of Human Resources* 22 (Fall 1987):551.

102. GAO, Report to the Chairman, Subcommittee on Employment and Productivity, Committee on Labor and Human Resources, U.S. Senate, *Emergency Jobs Act of 1983: Funds Spent Slowly, Few Jobs Created* (Washington, D.C.: GPO, December 1986):24-30.

103. GAO, *Emergency Jobs Act of 1983*, December 1986, 30-39.

104. GAO, *Emergency Jobs Act of 1983*, December 1986, 27.

105. Thomas Janoski, "The Political Economy of Unemployment: Active Labor Market Policy in West Germany and the United States," Doctoral Dissertation, Duke University, 1986, 217-249.

106. GAO, Report to the Chairman, Subcommittee on Employment and Productivity, Committee on Labor and Human Resources, U.S. Senate, *Emergency Jobs Act of 1983: Projects Funded in the Lawrence-Haverhill, Massachusetts, Area* (Washington, D.C.: GPO, December 1985), 24.

107. Gary Burtless, "Inequality in America: Where Do We Stand?," *Brookings Review* 107 (Summer 1987):11.

108. Frank Levy, "The Middle Class: Is It Really Vanishing?" *Brookings Review* 5 (Summer 1987):21; Richard J. Butler and James B. McDonald, "Income Inequality in the United States, 1948-1980" in *Research in Labor Economics*, vol. 8, part a, ed. Richard G. Ehrenberg (Greenwich, CT: JAI Press, 1986), 91-98; Bennett Harrison and Barry Bluestone, "The Dark Side of Labor Market 'Flexibility': Falling Wages and Growing Income Inequality in America," *Labor Market Analysis and Employment Planning*, working paper no. 17 (Geneva: ILO, October 1987), 20-25.

109. Frank Levy, "The Middle Class," 1987, 18.

110. U.S., Council of Economic Advisors, *Economic Report of the President with the Annual Report of the Council of Economic Advisors* (Washington, DC: GPO, 1987), Table B-29.

111. Burtless, "Inequality in America," 1987: 15.

112. Harrison and Bluestone, "The Dark Side of Labour Market 'Flexibility,'" ILO, 1987, 8; Robert G. Sheets, Stephen Nord, and John J. Phelps, *The Impact of Service Industries on Underemployment in Metropolitan Economies* (Lexington, MA: Lexington Books, 1987), 58-62.

113. Helen Ginsburg, *Full Employment and Public Policy: The United States and Sweden* (Lexington, MA: Lexington Books, 1983), 78.

114. Arnold J. Heidenheimer, Hugh Heclo, and Carolyn Teich Adams, *Comparative Public Policy: The Politics of Social Choice in Europe and America* (New York: St. Martin's Press, 1975), 262.

115. Thomas Janoski, "Political Economy or Demographic Reaction: Active Labor Market Policy in the U.S. and West Germany from 1950 to 1984," unpublished paper, Duke University, 1986.

116. Janoski, "Political Economy or Demographic Reaction," 1986.

117. Janoski, "Political Economy or Demographic Reaction," 1986.

Bibliography

Abraham, Katherine G. "Help-Wanted Advertising, Job Vacancies, and Unemployment." *Brookings Papers on Economic Activity.* 1987, 1:207-243.

Barnow, Burt S. "The Impact of CETA Programs on Earnings," *Journal of Human Resources* 22 (Winter 1987): 157-193.

Beale, Calvin L. and Glenn V. Fuguitt. "Metropolitan and Nonmetropolitan Growth Differentials in the United States Since 1980." Center for Demography and Ecology. Working paper 85-6. Madison, WI: CDE, 1985.

Bednarzik, Robert W. "An Examination of the Shift in Jobs from the Goods to the Service Sector in the U.S." Paper presented at OECD meeting, Tokyo, 15-19 June 1987.

_____. "Involuntary Part-time Work: A Cyclical Analysis." *Monthly Labor Review* 98 (September 1975): 12-18.

Belous, Richard S. "Flexibility and American Labour Markets: The Evidence and Implications." Labour Market Analysis and Employment Planning. Working paper no. 14. Geneva: ILO, June 1987.

Blau, Francine and Marianne Ferber. *The Economics of Women, Men and Work.* Englewood Cliffs, N.J.: Prentice Hall, 1986.

Burtless, Gary. "Inequality in America: Where Do We Stand?" *Brookings Review* 107 (Summer 1987): 9-17.

Butler, Richard J. and James B. McDonald. "Income Inequality in the United States, 1948-1980." In *Research in Labor Economics*, vol. 8, part a, edited by Richard G. Ehrenberg. Greenwich, CT: JAI Press, 1986.

Cantor, Richard and John Wenninger. "Current Labor Market Trends and Inflation." *Federal Reserve Bank of New York Quarterly Review* 12 (Autumn 1987): 36-48.

Culp, Jerome and Bruce Dunson. "Brothers of a Different Color." In *The Black Youth Employment Crisis*, edited by R. Freeman and H.J. Holzer. Chicago: The University of Chicago Press, 1986.

DeBoer, Larry and Michael Seeborg. "The Female-Male Unemployment Differential: Effects of Change in Industry Employment." *Monthly Labor Review* 107 (November 1984): 8-14.

Garn, Harvey A. *Labor Market Analysis and Public Policy.* Washington, DC: Urban Institute, 1970.

Ginsburg, Helen. *Full Employment and Public Policy: The United States and Sweden.* Lexington, MA: Lexington Books, 1983.

Gray, H. Peter, Thomas Pugel and Ingo Walter. *International Trade, Employment and*

123

Structural Adjustment: The United States. Geneva: ILO, 1986.

Grossman, Jonathan. *The Department of Labor*. New York: Praeger, 1973.

Gueron, Judith. *Work-Welfare Programs*. New Directions for Program Evaluation. No. 37. San Francisco: Jossey-Bass, 1988.

Harris, Louis & Associates, Inc. *The ICD Survey of Disabled Americans: Bringing Disabled Americans into the Mainstream*. Study 854009. New York: International Center for the Disabled and National Council on the Handicapped, 1986.

Harrison, Bennett and Barry Bluestone. "The Dark Side of Labour Market 'Flexibility': Falling Wages and Growing Income Inequality in America." Labour Market Analysis and Employment Planning. Working paper no. 17. Geneva: ILO, 1987.

Haveman, Robert, V. Halberstadt, and R.V. Burkhauser. *Public Policy Toward Disabled Workers*. New York: Cornell University Press, 1984.

Heidenheimer, Arnold J., Hugh Heclo, and Carolyn Teich Adams. *Comparative Public Policy: The Politics of Social Choice in Europe and America*. New York: St. Martin's Press, 1975.

Horvarth, Francis W. "The Pulse of Economic Change: Displaced Workers of 1981-1985." *Monthly Labor Review* 107 (June 1987): 3-12.

Howe, Wayne J. "Education and Demographics: How Do They Affect Unemployment Rates?" *Monthly Labor Review* 111 (January 1988): 3-9.

_____. "Temporary Help Workers: Who They Are, What Jobs   They Hold." *Monthly Labor Review* 109 (November 1986): 45-47.

Janoski, Thomas. "Political Economy or Demographic Reaction: Active Labor Market Policy in the U.S. and West Germany from 1950 to 1984." Unpublished paper, Duke University, 1986.

_____. "The Political Economy of Unemployment: Active Labor Market Policy in West Germany and the United States." Doctoral Dissertation, Duke University, 1986.

Johannesson, Jan. "On the Composition and Outcome of Swedish Labor Market Policy: 1970-1987." Stockholm: EFA, 1987.

Levy, Frank. "The Middle Class: Is It Really Vanishing?" *Brookings Review* 5 (Summer 1987): 17-21.

Long, David A. "Analyzing Social Program Production: An Assessment of Supported Work for Youths." *Journal of Human Resources* 22 (Fall 1987): 551-562.

Long, Larry. *Migration and Residential Mobility in the United States*. New York: Russell Sage Foundation, 1988.

March, James G. and Herbert A. Simon. *Organizations*. New York: John Wiley, 1958.

Marshall, F. Ray, Allan G. King, and Vernon M. Briggs, Jr. *Labor Economics*. Homewood, Illinois: Irwin, 1980.

Martin, Philip L. *Labor Displacement and Public Policy*. Lexington, MA: Lexington Books, 1983.

Mathematica Policy Research, Inc. *Digest of Data on Persons with Disabilities*. Washington, DC: Congressional Research Service, 1984.

Nathan, Richard P., R.F. Cook, and V.L. Rawlins, *Public Service Employment*. Washington, D.C.: Brookings, 1981.

New York Times. 9 July 1986, 20 October 1986, 25 December 1987, 16 March 1988.

Okun, Arthur M. "Potential GNP: Its Measurements and Significance." In *Economic*

Policymaking, edited by Joseph Pechman. Cambridge, MA: Massachusetts Institute of Technology, 1983.

Organization for Economic Cooperation and Development. *Employment Outlook.* September 1986, September 1987.

_____. *Flexibility in the Labour Market: The Current Debate.* Paris: OECD, 1986.

Personick, Valerie A. "Industry Output and Employment through the End of the Century." *Monthly Labor Review* 110 (September 1987): 30-45.

Peters, B. Guy. "The United States: Absolute Change and Relative Stability." In *Public Employment in Western Nations* edited by R. Rose. Cambridge: Cambridge University Press, 1985.

Rytina, Nancy F. "Occupational Changes and Tenure, 1981." *Tenure and Occupational Change, 1981,* Bureau of Labor Statistics Bulletin 2162. Washington, DC: GPO, January 1983, 4-8.

Schmid, Gunther. *Labour Market Policy in Transition.* Stockholm: EFA, 1988.

Seeborg, Michael and Larry DeBoer. "The Narrowing Male-Female Unemployment Differential." *Growth and Change* 12(Spring 1987): 24-37.

Sehgal, Ellen. "Occupational Mobility and Job Tenure in 1983." *Monthly Labor Review* 107 (October 1984): 18-23.

Shapiro, Robert Y., et al. "The Polls—A Report: Employment and Social Welfare." *Public Opinion Quarterly* 51 (Summer 1987): 268-281.

Sheets, Robert G., Stephen Nord, and John J. Phelps. *The Impact of Service Industries on Underemployment in Metropolitan Economies.* Lexington, MA: Lexington Books, 1987.

Taylor, Betsy and Robert W. Bednarzik. "U. S. Treatment of Displaced Workers." Unpublished paper, August 1986.

U.S. Congress. *Congressional Quarterly Weekly Report* 46 (2 January 1988).

_____. House. Committee on Ways and Means. *Background Material and Data on Programs within the Jurisdiction of the Committee on Ways and Means.* 100th Cong., 1st sess., 6 March 1987.

_____. House. Committee on Ways and Means. *Background Material and Data on Programs within the Jurisdiction of the Committee on Ways and Means.* 101st Cong., 1st sess., 15 March 1989.

_____. House. Testimony of John G. Bickerman of the Center for Budget and Policy Priorities. Subcommittee on Employment and Housing. Committee on Government Operations. *Changes in the Unemployment Insurance System: Is the Safety Net Eroding?* 99th Cong., 2d sess., 22 May 1986, 3-22.

_____. House. Testimony of Wayne Vroman of the Urban Institute. Subcommittee on Employment and Housing. Committee on Government Operations. *Changes in the Unemployment Insurance Program: Is the Safety Net Eroding?* 99th Cong., 2d sess., 22 May 1986, 23-43.

_____. Senate. Committee on Labor and Human Resources. *Work and Welfare.* 100th Cong., 1st sess., 21 January and 3 and 4 February 1987.

_____. Senate. *Congressional Record.* 99th Cong. 2d sess., 1986. Vol. 132.

U.S. Council of Economic Advisors. *Economic Report of the President.* Washington, DC: Government Printing Office, January 1987.

U.S. Department of Commerce. Bureau of the Census. *Consumer Income*. Current Population Reports. Population Characteristics, Series P-60, 1979.
_____. Bureau of the Census. *Geographical Mobility*. Current Population Reports. Population Characteristics, Series P-20, 1960-86.
_____. Bureau of the Census. *Statistical Abstract of the United States*. Washington, DC: Government Printing Office, various editions, 1970-1988.
_____. Bureau of Economic Analysis. *Survey of Current Business* 63(July 1983) through 67(July 1987).
U.S. Department of Labor. Bureau of Labor Statistics. "Children of Working Mothers." Bulletin 2158. March 1983.
_____. *Employment and Earnings* 18 (January 1971) through 35(March 1988).
_____. *Employment in Perspective: Minority Workers*. No. 699, 1983; Nos. 730, 744, 746, and 748, 1987.
_____. *Employment in Perspective: Women in the Labor Force*. Nos. 730 and 731, 1986; Nos. 739 and 743, 1987.
_____. *Employment Situation*. November 1987.
_____. *Handbook of Labor Statistics*. Bulletin 2217. Washington, DC: GPO, 1985.
_____. "Job Search of Recipients of Unemployment Insurance." *Monthly Labor Review* 102 (February 1979): 49-54.
_____. *Labor Force Statistics Derived from the Current Population Survey: A Databook*, vol. 1. Washington, DC: Government Printing Office, September 1982.
_____. "Linking Employment Problems to Economic Status." Bulletin 2282. Washington, DC: GPO, August 1987.
_____. *Monthly Labor Review* 107 (January 1984) through 111(December 1988).
_____. *News*. 85-25, January 1985; 85-355, October 1985; 86-125, March 1986; 87-67, February 1987; 87-345, August 1987; 97-415, September 1987; 87-452, October 1987; 87-536, December 1987; and 88-76, February 1988.
_____. "Projections 2000: The Changing Labor Force." *Occupational Outlook Quarterly* 31 (Fall 1987): 4-13.
U.S. Department of Labor. Employment and Training Division. *Employment and Training Handbook*. No. 394. Washington, DC: GPO, 1983.
_____. *Unemployment Insurance Financial Data*. Washington, DC: GPO, 1983.
U.S. General Accounting Office. Briefing Report to the Chairman. Committee on Labor and Human Resources. U.S. Senate. *Job Corps: Its Costs, Employment Outcomes and Service to the Public*. Washington, DC: GAO, July 1986.
_____. Briefing Report to the Chairman. Committee on Post Office and Civil Service. U.S. House of Representatives. *Federal Workforce: New Authority to Make and Extend Temporary Appointments*. Washington, DC: GAO, July 1986.
_____. Fact Sheet for the Chairman. Subcommittee on Civil Service, Post Office and General Services. Committee on Governmental Affairs. U.S. Senate. *Federal Workforce: Views on Need to Offer Health Insurance to Temporary Employees*. Washington, DC: GAO, June 1987.

_____. Fact Sheet for the Committee on Finance. U.S. Senate. *Work and Welfare: Analysis of AFDC Employment Programs in Four States*. Washington, DC: GAO, January 1988.

_____. Report to the Chairman. Subcommittee on Employment and Productivity. Committee on Labor and Human Resources. U.S. Senate. *Emergency Jobs Act of 1983: Funds Spent Slowly, Few Jobs Created*. Washington, D.C.: GAO, December 1986.

_____. Report to the Chairman. Subcommittee on Employment and Productivity. Committee on Labor and Human Resources. U.S. Senate. *Emergency Jobs Act of 1983: Projects Funded in the Lawrence-Haverhill, Massachusetts, Area*. Washington, D.C.: GAO, December 1985.

_____. Report to the Chairman. Subcommittee on Employment Opportunities. Committee on Education and Labor. U.S. House of Representatives. *CETA Programs for Disadvantaged Adults—What Do We Know about Their Enrollees, Services, and Effectiveness?* Washington, DC: GAO, June 1982.

_____. Report to the Congress. *Dislocated Workers: Local Programs and Outcomes Under the Job Training Partnership Act*. Washington, DC: GAO, March 1987.

U.S. National Council on the Handicapped. *Toward Independence*. Washington, DC: GPO, 1986.

U.S. Social Security Administration, *Social Security Bulletin* 51 (February 1988).

The Washington Post. National Weekly Edition, 9 February 1987.

Wise, Lois Recascino. "Dimensions of Public Sector Pay Administration." *Review of Public Personnel Administration* 8 (Summer 1988): 61-83.

Index

War on poverty, 97
Washington, D.C., 85
Welfare recipients, 94, 102–104
West Germany, 7, 12, 15, 20, 25, 25(table), 26, 26(table), 27, 29, 41, 71, 113
West Virginia, 84, 105(table)
WIN. See Work Incentive Program
Women, 114
  black, 114
  CETA participants, 101
  and childbearing, 28
  as discouraged workers, 83, 83–84(tables)
  earnings vs. men's, 58, 61(table 4.5), 101
  as head of household, 109–110, 109(table)
  and job tenure, 67
  and low-paying jobs, 60
  and manufacturing, 76
  and mobility, 65
  and occupational mobility, 63
  participation rate in work force, 27–28
  and part-time work, 32–33
  and poverty, 109–110
  and temporary work, 36
  training assistance for, 95–96
  white vs. non-white earnings, 59–60
  See also Work force, women in
Workers' Compensation, 10, 13(table)
Work force
  age composition, 26–27, 27(table), 28, 31(table), 48, 68
  black males in, 29
  blacks in, 29, 32(table)
  college graduates in, 29, 31
  disabled in, 76–77, 77(fig.), 78(table)

dislocated workers, 17–18, 17(table), 102, 103(table)
displaced workers, 78–80, 80–81(tables), 99
economically disadvantaged, 17, 17(table), 18
and education, 29, 31, 32(table)
federal civilian, 35
growth in, 25–26, 26(table)
Hispanics in, 24, 29, 31, 32(table), 49, 115
Hispanic women in, 29
insured vs. uninsured in, 90(table)
men in, 28, 29, 30(figs.), 31(table), 49
minority youths, 115
mobility of, 61–67
new entrants/re-entrants, 70, 70(table), 87
numbers in, 23, 24
participation rates. See Participation rates
and post World War II birth cohort, 25, 26
racial minorities, 13
summer youth, 17, 17(table)
teenagers in, 33
whites in, 13, 24, 32(table)
women in, 27–28, 29, 30(figs.), 31(table), 49, 77, 82. See also Women
in year 2000, 24
young adults in, 29, 35, 115
See also Labor market
Work Incentive Program (WIN), 18, 94, 102, 104(tables)
Works Progress Administration, 97
World War II, 97

Youth joblessness programs, 97, 105–106